D0803979

STORIES

BEHIND THE BEST-LOVED

SONGS

of

CHRISTMAS

Also by Ace Collins

STORIES

BEHIND THE BEST-LOVED

SONGS

of

CHRISTMAS

ACE COLLINS

ILLUSTRATIONS BY CLINT HANSEN

ZONDERVAN™

GRAND RAPIDS, MICHIGAN 49530

ZONDERVAN™

Stories Behind the Best-Loved Songs of Christmas
Copyright © 2001 by Andrew Collins

Requests for information should be addressed to:

Zondervan, *Grand Rapids, Michigan 49530*

ISBN 0-310-26448-0

Illustrations by Clint Hansen

Interior design by Todd Sprague

Printed in the United States of America

04 05 06 07 08 09/❖ DC/ 10 9 8 7 6 5 4 3 2 1

For Terry,
who, in a small rural church
on a snowy night,
brought "O Holy Night" to life.
Thanks for all you have given me
over the years.
Love,
Ace

CONTENTS

FOREWORD

There is a treasure of inspiration to be found in these pages. If you love Christmas, then this book is going to bless you time and time again. You will laugh and cry, and history will come to life. You will learn and understand things you didn't know before, giving you a much richer grasp of the music that makes this season so very special. You will probably also want to rush out and tell someone you know one of these stories.

Those who know me well know that Christmas is my favorite time of the year. I love shopping, wrapping gifts, decorating, and even the hustle and bustle that goes with the season. But above all the other traditions, I love the music of Christmas.

For me, music brings Christmas to life. Songs about the birth of Jesus transport me to the first Christmas. A carol that describes snow makes me feel the chill. When I hear the story of a shunned reindeer, I feel sorry for him. I guess because these songs offer wonderful memories along with beautiful music, I treasure the times I get to sing them at home, in church, and on the stage. To me, each one of these special songs is a pretty package that I get to unwrap again every year; and now, thanks to this book, each one of these musical packages contains a newly discovered surprise that makes it even

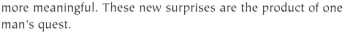

more meaningful. These new surprises are the product of one man's quest.

Ace Collins is not only one of my closest friends, he is my favorite writer and the best storyteller I have ever known. In this book, he has touched me like never before. To know the background on these inspirational Christmas songs has changed my perspective on Christmas itself. I will never again sing any of these carols without being transported back to the place and time it was written.

Stories Behind the Best-Loved Songs of Christmas is a book that will bring the Christmas season into sharper focus for you. You will find out why I now wish my friends a "mighty" Christmas, how a tiny bell made a movie unforgettable, and why one of the most spiritual songs I have ever sung was once banned by the church. Yet more than simple information and holiday trivia, these stories will enlighten and inspire you in ways I can't begin to explain. I can only say that after reading this book, I believe that Christmas—its roots and traditions and music— will mean so much more to you.

Thank you, Ace, for answering the call and bringing these stories to the world. Your gift of this book helps all of us to remember the true reason for the season and the inspiration behind the music that brings Christmas to life each year. There is no doubt that reading and rereading *Stories Behind the Best-Loved Songs of Christmas* will be a central part of my Christmas for years to come. I can hardly wait to share this book with everyone I know and love.

—*Louise Mandrell*

ANGELS, FROM THE REALMS OF GLORY

ngels, from the Realms of Glory"—possibly the best-written, sacred Christmas carol of all time—helped launch a revolution that continues to impact millions of lives today. At its heart is its writer, an Irishman born in November of 1771.

James Montgomery was born in Irvine, Ayrshire, Scotland. Montgomery's father, John, was an Irish Moravian missionary. When his parents were called to evangelistic work in the West Indies, the child was sent to a Moravian community in Ballymena, County Antrim, Ireland. By the time he was seven, James was at Fulneck Seminary, Yorkshire, England. Five years later, the parents James hardly knew died on the mission field.

Perhaps because of the distance from and the tragic loss of his parents, Montgomery never was very interested in his schooling. Flunking out of seminary, he became a baker's assistant for a short time. By the age of twenty, the young

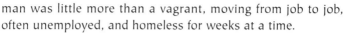

man was little more than a vagrant, moving from job to job, often unemployed, and homeless for weeks at a time.

Montgomery's only interest was writing. He spent what little money he had on pencils and paper, taking hours to compose poetic odes on everything from loneliness to faith. Though no publisher was interested in his work, the radical editor of the *Sheffield Register* saw something in the young man's raw talent. For the next two years Montgomery got paid to do what he most loved to do—write stories. He also learned firsthand about the hardships of being an Irishman under English rule. At the age of twenty-three, when the newspaper's owner was run out of town for writing radical editorials concerning Irish freedom, the missionary's son took over the *Register*.

In an attempt to quell the British government's wrath, Montgomery changed the paper's name to the *Sheffield Iris*. Yet he didn't change its editorial stance. Just as his parents had strongly rebelled against the strict rules and rituals of England's official church, James was bent on carrying on a written war for Ireland's freedom. At about that time, he also became an active leader in the abolitionist movement. His fiery editorial stance twice landed him in prison. Yet each time he was released, he returned to the *Iris* and continued his printed war for freedom on all fronts.

When Montgomery was not waging an editorial crusade against English rule and slavery, he was reading his Bible in an attempt to understand the power that motivated his parents' lives and ultimately led to their deaths. In time, his Scripture study and rebellious zeal would blend and send the young man on a new mission. One of the first hints of this change was revealed on Christmas Eve 1816.

Irishmen, who hated all things British, probably carefully studied the newspaper each day, hoping to find some Montgomery-penned passage that would inspire more to join their

Angels, from the realms of glory,
Wing your flight o'er all the earth;
Ye who sang creation's story,
Now proclaim Messiah's birth.

Chorus:
Come and worship, come and worship,
Worship Christ the newborn King.

Shepherds in the fields abiding,
Watching o'er your flocks by night,
God with man is now residing,
Yonder shines the infant Light.

Chorus

Sages, leave your contemplations,
Brighter visions beam afar;
Seek the great Desire of nations,
Ye have seen His natal star.

Chorus

Saints before the altar bending,
Watching long in hope and fear,
Suddenly the Lord, descending,
In His temple shall appear.

Chorus

revolution. It is certain that local government officials who read the *Iris* often wished to nail the man who was so often a thorn in their side. Yet on December 24, 1816, readers discovered a different stance from the fiery editor. On that day, his editorial did not divide Irish from English, but rather brought everyone who read the *Iris* closer together.

Written in the same poetic verse that Montgomery had employed during the aimless wanderings of his youth, "Nativity"—what would eventually become the carol "Angels, from the Realms of Glory"—told the story of angels proclaiming the birth of a Savior for all people, English and Irish, rich and poor, Anglican and Moravian. Eloquent, beautiful, and scripturally sound, Montgomery soon touched more lives for Christ with the stroke of his pen than his parents did in all their years of missionary work.

Still, when read between the lines, there was a bit of social commentary in "Nativity." A verse long-deleted from the carol speaks of a society that needs to right some wrongs. That lost stanza also reveals the writer's personal journey in finding purpose and meaning in his own life:

> *Sinners, wrung with true repentance,*
> *Doomed for guilt to endless pains,*
> *Justice now revokes the sentence;*
> *Mercy calls you. Break your chain.*

As Montgomery would soon find out, his poem *would* break chains, but not those he had envisioned. The impact of "Nativity" would actually foreshadow the writer's future, since he would come to revolutionize music and thinking in the English church.

As often is the case with inspired work, irony stepped in and took an important role in revealing "Nativity" to a mass audience.

The Irish revolutionary's poem might have been forgotten if not for an Englishman. It was a member of the English establishment, the same group against which Montgomery had long fought, that would become the agent in making his poem a worldwide favorite.

Henry Smart, the son of a music publisher, had given up a successful law career to become one of England's finest organists and composers. Like Montgomery, he was a revolutionary, only his cause was bringing new and beautiful music to English congregations, something that often involved bitter conflicts. Many traditionalists wanted nothing in church services but the simple chants that had been a part of worship for hundreds of years. They often argued that the members of the congregation were merely spectators and should not be involved in the important facets of worship. Smart, however, felt that God spoke to every man and woman and that worship should be a joyful, corporate experience.

In the face of ridicule, Smart published new songbooks with harmonized melodies. When people heard his harmonies, they demanded that his work be used by the church. Bowing to the will of the people—and realizing that other Protestant denominations had already begun using this "new" musical style—the Church of England allowed the composer's ideas to take root. It is no exaggeration to say that Smart is to harmonized church music what Bach is to the German chorale.

Yet the fact that Smart *saw* the need for new excitement in worship was ironic. By the age of eighteen, Smart was going blind. He probably couldn't have even read the poem that James Montgomery had written on Christmas Eve, 1816. But somewhere, some twenty years after it had been written, the composer listened to the Irishman's words. Inspired by the wisdom, power, fire, and beauty he saw in "Nativity," Smart composed a tune to go with the poem. When published, the Montgomery/Smart collaboration had a different title and a new, vibrant life. "Angels, from the Realms of Glory" would not only be welcomed as a new Christmas carol, it would soon become one of the songs that opened the door for a new, joyful, and uplifting musical style in hundreds of English churches.

But even before Smart had married his music to Montgomery's poem, Montgomery had lost interest in the Irish revolution. As he grew to fully understand his parents' calling, he returned to the Moravian church and became an avid worker for missions. He also began to write hymns, ultimately composing more than four hundred. With the aid of Henry Smart, he led a quieter rebellion, bringing a festive, personal style of music into church services that made the congregation an active part of worship.

A music critic once wrote, "For comprehensiveness, appropriateness of expression, force and elevation of sentiment, 'Angels, from the Realms of Glory' may challenge comparison with any hymn that was ever written, in any language or country." Therefore, it seems appropriate that the strong faith that was evident in every word, line, and verse not only sustained the song's remarkable writer on his often difficult and solitary journey through life, but also helped open the church door for a more joyful worship experience.

Always looking at his own life and experiences for inspiration, Montgomery once wrote in an inspirational poem that he meant to set to music:

Beyond this vale of tears,
There is a life above,
Unmeasured by the flight of years;
And all that life is love.

Montgomery continued to write hymns until the day he died in 1854. By that time, the man twice imprisoned by England for his beliefs had heard his "Angels, from the Realms of Glory" sung in the Anglican churches of London. And the revolution begun in an Irishman's newspaper eventually touched people both throughout England and far beyond her borders.

ANGELS WE HAVE HEARD ON HIGH

*M*any images accompany Christmas—fun and frolic, snow and decorations, laughter and family gatherings—images so ingrained in most people's minds that they find it difficult to imagine the holiday any other way. Yet, in truth, Christmas only recently became the festive holiday we now cherish. For almost fifteen hundred years, the observation of the birth of Jesus was not recognized on every street corner but left to divinely called men who led a hard and demanding life, toiling in poverty and serving people who understood little about the most elementary facets of Scripture and the life of the soul. Yet these men stayed the course and left their fingerprints on every church of every denomination in the world today.

Monks were and still are solitary men, dedicating every ounce of their being to the Lord and giving up their own families to serve the family of God. Their voices were often the only ones who told of the birth of Christ and their lives the only example of Christian faith. Even to those who knew them, monks were mysterious figures. Their world was one of sacrifice, their sense of duty second only to their humble spirit. Yet from this spirit and life came one of the most beautiful and soaring carols of Christmas.

Much like the lives of most monks, "Angels We Have Heard on High" is a song steeped in great mystery. Unlike other carols whose writers are unknown but whose origins can be clearly traced to a certain time or certain place, this song seemingly appeared out of the air. Because the first to sing "Angels We Have Heard on High" lived in nineteenth century France, many believe that it must have originated there. In fact, most sources today call it a French carol. Yet even that assumption is often called into question by songologists. What can be stated with absolute certainty is that this Christmas song must have been penned by a person who had a professional knowledge of the Bible and an incredible gift for taking Scripture and reshaping it into verse. This fact, combined with the use of Latin in the song's chorus—making it a macaronic carol—seems to indicate that a monk or priest from the Catholic church was more than likely responsible for writing "Angels We Have Heard on High."

Because the first published versions of the song used French for the verses, many have naturally assumed that its writer was a priest from France. Yet there is evidence that at least part of this great Christmas hymn was sung before Christianity took deep root in western Europe. A portion of the carol was used in early Christian church services even before the Roman Empire adopted Christianity as the state religion.

"Angels We Have Heard on High" was first published in 1855 in the French songbook *Nouveau recueil de cantiques,* and records indicate that the song had been used in church masses for more than fifty years before that publication. During those five decades the lyrics were coupled with the melody that is still used today. Except for the verses translated into languages other than French, today the song is sung just as it was a hundred and fifty years ago. Yet for maybe a thousand years or more before that, monks probably sang this same song as they celebrated the birth of the Savior. The story may well be as old as the church itself.

The song's four verses embrace the angels' visit to the lowly shepherds and the shepherds' response. For many biblical scholars, the angels coming to men who worked menial jobs in the fields and informing *them* of the birth of the Son of God symbolizes that Christ came for all people, rich or poor, humble or powerful. The angels' words in Luke 2, "Fear not: for, behold, I bring you good tidings of great joy, which shall be to all people," paired with Jesus' own parables concerning shepherds and their flocks, symbolizes that it would be the common man and not kings or religious leaders who would first carry the story of Jesus' life to the masses.

But while the shepherds' story of why they came to see the babe in the manger is easily identified in all the stanzas, for many who sing this old song, the chorus is an enigma. "Gloria in excelsis Deo" means, in English, "Glory to God in the highest," a phrase that played an important part of worship at church masses dating back to 130 A.D. During that period, Pope Telesphorus issued a decree that on the day of the Lord's birth all churches should have special evening services. He also ordered that, at these masses, after the reading of certain Scripture or the conclusion of specific prayers, the congregation should always sing the words "Gloria in excelsis Deo." Historical church documents reveal that monks carried this executive order throughout the land and that by the third century it was a practice used by most churches at Christmas services.

It can be argued that if the chorus was written within a hundred years of Christ's birth, the roots of "Angels We Have Heard

Angels we have heard on high,
Sweetly singing o'er the plains,
And the mountains, in reply,
Echoing their joyous strains.

Chorus:
Gloria in excelsis Deo,
Gloria in excelsis Deo.

Shepherds, why this jubilee?
Why your joyous strains prolong?
Say what may the tidings be,
Which inspire your heav'nly song?

Chorus

Come to Bethlehem and see
Him whose birth the angels sing;
Come, adore on bended knee
Christ the Lord, the newborn King.

Chorus

See within a manger laid,
Jesus, Lord of heav'n and earth!
Mary, Joseph, lend your aid,
With us sing our Savior's birth.

Chorus

on High" might go back to someone who actually knew Jesus when he walked on earth. Though unproved, it is a very interesting and inspiring idea and ties in to the selfless image of a called member of the clergy bringing faith alive in order to spread the message of Jesus Christ's birth, life, and death.

Another facet of this carol that would seem to tie at least its chorus to the very early Catholic church is the range of notes found in the chorus. While most modern carols move up and down and cover at least an octave and a half, thus testing the upper or lower limits of the average singer, the phrase "Gloria in excelsis Deo" barely moves at all. In addition, the melody used by the song never strays more than one octave and the verse moves through only six notes. This simplicity seems to tie the melody to early chants used by monks and taught to their congregations.

Webster defines a chant as "singing or speaking in a monotone to a hymnlike repetitive melody." Using this approach, important elements of worship were passed on from person to person and generation to generation in the oral tradition. In a day when few read words—much less music—chants helped keep the gospel alive among the common people. Of all the carols born in the chanting tradition, "Angels We Have Heard on High," was one of the easiest and least challenging, despite the fact that the word "gloria" covers three measures and hits almost twenty different notes. Unlike others, which failed to inspire as they taught, this song lifted hearts while telling the story.

It embraced the spirit that a called man of God would have felt as he gave up everything to serve his Lord.

So why has this carol of unknown origin remained so popular for so long? Though the tune may be considered monotonous, when the simple text is read it becomes obvious that few Christmas songs so fully describe the joy that the world felt when a Savior was born in Bethlehem. The lyrics don't just ask the singer to lift up his or her eyes and heart in wonder and observe the beauty of what God has given the world, they demand it. There can be no doubt that whoever wrote "Angels We Have Heard on High" not only believed the words found in the Bible, but relished that belief.

Ultimately, it is the sensitive retelling of the angel-shepherd story that carries this song and has made it one of the world's most popular Christmas carols. As Kenneth W. Osbeck wrote in his devotional book, *Amazing Grace,* "The Bible teaches that angels are the ministering servants of God and that they are continually being sent to help and protect us, the heirs of salvation." "Angels We Have Heard on High" speaks of the incredible, special relationship between heaven and earth, God and man, like few songs ever have. It embraces one of the most important elements of faith just as the shepherds embraced the Good News they were given two thousand years ago.

The mystery of who wrote this song points back to the lives of *all* those who are called to spread the gospel, to keep the story alive, to provide a means for people everywhere to hear and know the message that came to earth on that first Christmas. One of those nameless servants wrote this song to share the story with others. Though he has long been forgotten, what he believed is alive in not only his song but in hundreds of millions of souls around the world. His prayer has been answered: the angels are still heard, the Savior still welcomed, and the soul still stirred.

AWAY IN A MANGER

*M*any Christmas carols are bathed in so many different legends that separating fact from legend becomes almost impossible. Such is the case with the beautiful and simple carol that tells the story of baby Jesus lying in a manger that first Christmas night.

Along with "Jesus Loves Me," "Away in a Manger" is one of the first songs that Christians teach children in Sunday school or church. With only three short verses and a very simple tune, it is no small wonder that little ones learn it long before they can read. The beautiful and serene picture painted in the carol's lyrics defines "peace on Earth" better than most books or sermons.

In 1887, American hymn writer James R. Murray entitled the tune to "Away in a Manger" as "Luther's Cradle Hymn." Murray further stated in his popular songbook, *Dainty Songs for Little Lads and Lasses*, that Martin Luther had not only written "Away in a Manger," but had sung it to his children each night before bed. As the song spread across a growing America and people began to sing it at home, in churches, and at schools, they often envisioned legions of German mothers rocking their babies to sleep each night with the strains of "Away in a Manger." As the song became more popular, some news reports even trumpeted the song's Teutonic heritage and the powerful inspiration that obviously could come from only the great Luther himself.

Ironically, not only did German mothers of this era *not* sing "Away in a Manger," they had never heard it until the song arrived in Europe from its country of origin, the United States. Where Murray got his misinformation on Luther remains a mystery, yet because of his outstanding reputation as a writer and publisher, the story stuck.

James R. Murray studied at the Musical Institute in North Reading, Massachusetts, under legendary teachers such as Lowell Mason, George Root, William Bradbury, and George Webb. His teachers marked their student as one of the finest young musical minds they had ever encountered. Yet Murray didn't stay the course in school. In 1862, in the midst of the American Civil War, Murray enlisted as an Army musician. During the darkest days of the war he wrote his first song, "Daisy Deane." Composed in a Virginia camp in 1863, the now forgotten ditty established Murray as a songwriter.

After the war ended and armed with a wealth of new material, Murray joined the Root and Cady publishing house in Chicago, Illinois, as editor of the *Song Messenger*. In 1881, Murray moved to Cincinnati, Ohio, to work for the John Church Company, editing the *Musical Visitor*. He also took charge of the company's publishing department. It was there that he happened upon "Away in a Manger."

Two years before Murray had printed "Away in a Manger" in his children's songbook, the General Council of the Evangelical

Lutheran Church in North America had published the song in their book *Little Children's Book: For School and Families.* Printed in Philadelphia, *Little Children's Book* listed no songwriter for the words to the song. The book stated that the tune—a much different one than that used by Murray—had been provided by J. E. Clark.

In truth, the first two verses of "Away in a Manger" were no doubt written by an anonymous American sometime in the mid-1800s. The song was probably passed down orally for years before it was picked up by the Lutheran editor. By the time it was first published, no one knew the identity of the composer.

In 1892, a man named Charles Hutchinson Gabriel became the music director of Chicago's Grace Methodist Episcopal Church. A poet, composer, and editor, it was in the Windy City that Gabriel wrote a legion of hymns—eventually more than seven hundred. The composer's work included such standards as "Way of the Cross," "My Savior's Love," "Higher Ground," and "I Stand Amazed in the Presence." It was while he was at Grace Church that Gabriel discovered not only the versions of "Away in a Manger" published by the Lutheran press and by James R. Murray, but also another, unknown version that contained a third verse. He published this new edition of the carol in *Gabriel's Vineyard Songs.*

Throughout the next two decades the popularity of "Away in a Manger" grew, as did the myth surrounding Luther's authorship of the piece. Illustrations were drawn and stories were told depicting Luther singing the song to German children. As the real author never came forward to dispute the growing legend, the facts of the carol's origination became more and more diluted.

Away in a manger, no crib for a
bed,
The little Lord Jesus laid down
His sweet head;
The stars in the sky looked down
where He lay,
The little Lord Jesus, asleep on
the hay.

The cattle are lowing, the Baby
awakes,
But little Lord Jesus, no crying
He makes;
I love Thee, Lord Jesus! look
down from the sky,
And stay by my cradle till morn-
ing is nigh.

Be near me, Lord Jesus, I ask
Thee to stay
Close by me forever, and love me,
I pray;
Bless all the dear children in Thy
tender care,
And fit us for heaven, to live with
Thee there.

During World War I, while Germany battled the United States, many groups began to sing the words to "Away in a Manger" with the old Scottish tune "Flow Gently Sweet Afton." This rendition might well have been a protest against any and all things German. Yet soon after the war, when most Americans had again embraced the original tune, a new songbook, *Words and Song*, gave a man named Carl Mueller credit as the musical composer of the song. Where the Boston publisher came up with Mueller's name is another unanswered question. Carl Mueller did not write the music to "Away in a Manger"; in fact, many believe that he didn't even exist.

In 1945, as Americans again battled Germany in a world war, American writer Richard S. Hill sorted through the now seventy-year-old mystery concerning the carol's origin. He determined that James R. Murray himself probably wrote the music long coupled with "Away in a Manger." Yet as Murray always took credit when he composed a song, it is doubtful that he would have deflected the credit to Martin Luther. It's more likely that Murray was given the song and simply adapted the existing German-influenced melody into four-part harmony for his book. It also seems likely that Murray received the story of Martin Luther writing the piece from the person who originally gave him the song.

Whoever he or she is, the unknown songwriter probably didn't live to see the song reach children the world over with its poignant message. Yet while the mystery of origination remains, the song's message, depicting the precious moment when a Savior came to Earth bringing peace, joy, and hope, is so strong and profound that it leaped from a single night, from a single household, to become one of the world's most beautiful Christmas messages in song. The picture *that* story paints is even more profound and riveting than that of Luther singing "Away in a Manger" in Deutsch to his children.

THE CHRISTMAS SONG

*O*ne of the most famous modern-day Christmas songs was written on one of the hottest California days on record. The song, which resulted from a collaboration between two of America's best singer-songwriters, has touched millions and made both men a fixture of every holiday season. In fact, for many, Nat King Cole singing "chestnuts roasting on an open fire"—the opening line of "The Christmas Song"—is one of the greatest moments in the history of music. Yet had it not been for a friend of Cole's named Mel Torme, who happened to drop by Cole's house with the song, Cole would never have had the chance to record it.

✳

Most baby boomers came to know Mel Torme from his appearances on the television series *Night Court*. Because of the show, "The Velvet Fog"—as he was called by fans—was seen as little more than an old, almost forgotten jazz singer. Torme relished playing up this false image of being a lounge lizard, though nothing could have been farther from the truth. Actually, Torme—a talented singer, songwriter, performer, and author—was one of the most ambitious men ever to walk onto a stage. His incredible catalog of credits continues to inspire people even after his death.

Torme grew up in show business. In the 1930s he was a child radio actor and vaudeville performer. By his teens he was already writing songs. When he was just sixteen, he quit high school to arrange music and play drums for the Marx Orchestra. Soon after, he worked with Frank Sinatra.

In 1944, Torme got together with two other talented musicians, Les Baxter and Henry Mancini, to form the vocal group the Mel-Tones. The trio was among the first of the jazz-influenced vocal groups. Five years later, Mel scored a solo number one hit with "Careless Hands" and quickly gained recognition as one of the top jazz artists in the world. Ethel Waters once said that Torme was "the only white man who sings with the soul of a black man." Soon, without realizing it, Mel—whose views of life and music were never complicated by racial prejudice—would serve as the key in opening a holiday door previously closed to African Americans.

Over the course of the next fifty years, Torme influenced generations of singers, sold millions of records, acted in dozens of movies and television shows, wrote a couple of best-selling books, arranged music for some of the greatest names in the business, and took a few years off to fly airplanes as a commercial pilot. Yet the one facet of his career that is often overlooked was his ability to write music. If the singer-songwriter hadn't decided to visit his friend Nat King Cole's house one hot summer day, "Born to Be Blue" would have probably gone down as his most remembered composition. But a July drive across Los Angeles changed all that forever.

Robert Wells, a lyricist, was one of Torme's best friends. They had written together for several years and had just been hired to produce the title songs for two movies, *Abie's Irish Rose* and *Magic Town*. When Mel arrived, rather than working on the assignments, he found Wells trying to drive off the California heat with fans and positive thinking. The fans were doing little good, and the positive thoughts—which consisted of writing down everything that reminded Wells of cold winters in New England—were only making Wells warmer. Many years later, Torme recalled what happened.

"I saw a spiral pad on his piano with four lines written in pencil. They started, 'Chestnuts roasting . . . Jack Frost nipping . . . Yuletide carols . . . Folks dressed up like Eskimos.' Bob didn't think he was writing a song lyric. He said he thought if he could immerse himself in winter he could cool off."

It had been chestnuts that started Wells's strange train of thought. He had seen his mother bring in a bag of them to stuff a turkey for dinner. Wells was thrown back to the days when he saw vendors selling chestnuts on New York City street corners. Yet while Wells was after nothing more than an attempt to "think cold," Mel caught a glimpse of a song in the phrases he had written. With the temperature in the nineties and both men sweating through their clothes, they got to work on what was to become a Christmas classic. It took just forty minutes. The assigned movie title songs were pushed aside as Wells and Torme climbed into a car and drove away to show off their latest song.

Torme knew all the great singers who worked in Los Angeles. They all liked and respected Mel's work and most of them palled around with the singer. So when Wells and Torme dropped by Nat King Cole's home uninvited, it didn't seem out of the ordinary. It was just old, friendly Mel being Mel. Yet the results of that visit were monumental. After a brief greeting, Torme took a seat at King's piano. On the hottest day of the year, Mel played the new Christmas number. It might not have cooled anyone off, but Cole was deeply impressed.

❄

Nat King Cole had begun his career as a jazz pianist and was one of the best. Yet by the 1940s, it was his smooth baritone that had mesmerized fans all over the world. Even at a time when some of the greatest balladeers in history ruled the airwaves, Cole stood out. The young black man from Chicago's voice and styling set him apart; his voice and stage presence earned him the nickname "King."

Cole's first huge hit came in 1946 with "I Love You for Sentimental Reasons." A long list of well-loved songs including "Mona Lisa," "Nature Boy," and "Too Young" followed. During an era when America was almost totally segregated, Cole's music erased the racial barriers, at least in music.

From the moment Torme stopped in at Cole's Los Angeles home and played "The Christmas Song" on his piano, Nat loved it. Sensing the song was a classic, he wanted to record it before Torme could offer it to anyone else. Within days, Cole had rearranged the song to suit his voice and pacing, and cut it for Capitol Records. His instincts about the song's potential were right. Released in October of 1946, the song stayed in the Top Ten for almost two months. Nat's hit charted again in 1947, 1949, 1950, and 1954. Though "The Christmas Song" would ultimately be recorded by more than a hundred other artists—including Bing Crosby, Judy Garland, and even Mel Torme himself—none could ever break Cole's "ownership rights." The song was instantly and forevermore a Nat King Cole classic.

No one thought about it at the time, but Cole's cut of Torme's song became the first American Christmas standard introduced by an African American. The success of that cut helped open the door for Lou Rawls, Ray Charles, and Ethel Waters to put their own spins on holiday classics. It gave black audiences a chance to hear their favorite stars sing the carols that they loved as deeply as all other Christians. Thanks to "The Christmas Song," for the first time in the commercial marketplace, Christmas was not reserved for "whites only."

❋

Cole died in his forties of cancer, while Torme lived into his seventies. Both men's careers hit incredible high notes, and their list of honors and accomplishments set them apart from most of their peers. But no moment for either was as memorable as when they were brought together by words that were meant to simply cool off a body on a hot day.

If there is such a thing as inspired magic, it can be found in this song. When people around the world hear Nat King Cole's rich baritone singing about cold noses and the wonderful carols that warm hearts at Christmas, they are blessed. The world has lost both Nat King Cole and Mel Torme, but their genius lives on in a song that continues to give millions the special spirit of the season—and the memory of a cool winter's eve—each and every year.

DO YOU HEAR WHAT I HEAR?

*T*he odds of Gloria Shayne and Noel Regney coming together were long at best. Yet somehow, although born worlds apart, a Frenchman and an American found each other in the middle of the world's busiest city and eventually teamed up to create a Christmas song that was truly inspired.

Noel Regney grew up in Europe with a deep love of music. As a young man, his effort to create new classical compositions was interrupted by the outbreak of World War II. Forced into the Nazi army, Regney soon escaped to his native France and joined a group of resistance fighters. Instead of writing peaceful music, he spent the rest of the war fighting to bring peace back to France.

After the war, it was music that brought Noel to the United States, and in the late 1950s he wandered into New York's Beverly Hotel. There, in the luxurious dining room, he saw a beautiful woman playing popular music on the piano. Though he spoke very little English, Noel was so enthralled that he boldly introduced himself to Gloria Shayne. Within a month, the man who spoke rudimentary English and the woman who didn't understand French, married.

On the surface, Noel and Gloria's union was very unique. What could an American woman, determined to write rock and roll, and a Frenchman, in the States to record classical music, have in common? Yet it would take the marriage of both their skill and insight, as well as their cultures and experience, to create a song that would cause millions around the world to stop, look, and listen.

By 1962, Noel had mastered English and been completely exposed to the world of American popular music, thanks in large part to Gloria's writing a huge rock and roll hit. Teen idol James Darren had cut Shayne's "Goodbye Cruel World" and took the number to the top of the charts. As her career took off, Gloria's passion for writing magnified. She spent hours each day at the piano beating out new material.

While Noel saw the financial potential of popular music and heard his wife playing it every day, he still wanted to create something beautiful that would last longer than just a quick trip up the charts. The inspiration that would utilize both the man's classical imagery and his wife's contemporary beat was to come from yet another war, this one fought a long way from the American city Regney now called home.

Noel had often prayed that World War II would be the war that would finally end all wars. He couldn't imagine anyone wanting to revisit the horrors he had viewed firsthand. Yet his prayer had been shattered in the '50s by the fighting in Korea. After Korea, Regney watched his native France, and then the United States, become entangled in a bloody jungle battle in Vietnam. As more and more young men were injured and killed, the Frenchman wondered if the world would ever find real peace.

Fighting the depression brought on by flashbacks to his own days as a Nazi soldier and then as a resistance fighter, coupled with the news he saw on television each day, Noel sought out something that would bring him peace of mind. In an effort to put his pain into perspective, he turned back to the one moment in time when he felt the Lord had given men a chance to live life without hate, fear, or conflict.

Picking up a pen, Regney wrote a poem about the first Christmas. Fighting through some of the most difficult moments he had ever faced, Noel pushed away his nightmarish memories of World War II, the news from Vietnam, and the current tension building between the U.S.S.R. and the U.S. — a pressure that seemed to be pushing the world into yet another war. As he concentrated on the events leading up to the birth of Jesus, the world around him grew strangely quiet.

His memories took Noel back to a scene of sheep walking through the beautiful green fields of his native France. He considered the innocence of a newly born lamb. This was a creature whose spirit man should emulate, an animal that surely the Creator himself had touched in a very special way. Thoughts of the lamb, and a child who might have cared for it, inspired Noel to write a poem that not only described peace on earth, but which also spoke of the peace that came to earth on that first Christmas night.

"When he finished," Gloria recalled, "Noel gave it to me and asked me to write the music. He said he wanted me to do it because he didn't want the song to be too classical. I read over the lyrics, then went shopping. I was going to Bloomingdale's when I thought of the first music line."

When Gloria returned home she discovered that she had inserted an extra note in her melody, causing her music to no longer fit Noel's lyrics. Listening to what his wife had composed,

Noel opted to add a word rather than risk losing what he considered one of the most beautiful melodies he had ever heard. So "Said the wind to the little lamb" became "Said the night wind to the little lamb." Not only did this addition keep the music intact, but the imagery of God speaking on the wind became even more wondrous. Yet when Gloria asked him to change one more line in the first verse, Noel balked.

"I told him that no one in this country would understand 'tail as big as a kite,'" Gloria explained. "Yet he wouldn't change that. As it turned out, he was right. It is a line that people dearly love."

The couple took the finished song to the Regent Publishing Company. Owned by the brothers of famed big band leader Benny Goodman, it was one of New York's best music houses. With Noel singing and Gloria playing, the song made its professional debut. Within minutes, Regent had contacted Harry Simeone. It was his group that had scored a huge Christmas hit four years before with "Little Drummer Boy." Simeone wanted to hear the song right away. Since the couple didn't have a demo, Gloria recalled that this created a major problem:

"Noel couldn't play and sing at the same time, and I had to go play for a commercial. I couldn't break my date, so he went by himself. When he got home he told me that he had botched it up."

Gloria and Noel had every reason to believe "Do You Hear What I Hear?" would not be recorded. Even if Regney had perfectly performed the song for Simeone, since the David Seville's comical Chipmunks had recently scored with a novelty Christmas number, it seemed that no one was looking for a spiritual holiday song. Both were shocked when, a few days later, the Harry Simeone Chorale recorded their touching work with plans to release it as a single.

"Noel hadn't had much success in his classical career," Gloria recalled, "and he wanted to do something meaningful and beautiful. In this song he did."

The couple could not have dared imagine the effect "Do You Hear What I Hear?" would have on the nation. At the height of the Cold War, millions, like Noel, were yearning for peace and hope. This carol's combination of words and music powerfully voiced those prayers. Newspaper stories of the time wrote of drivers hearing it for the first time on the radio and pulling their cars off the road to listen. It seemed that the song didn't just touch the world; it made people stop, look, and listen.

In 1963, "Do You Hear What I Hear?" became a Christmas standard when it was recorded by Bing Crosby. It was sung by church choirs, became an integral part of television specials, and inspired numerous magazine features and even Christmas sermons.

"We couldn't believe it," Gloria admitted. "So many people wrote us to tell how much the song meant to them. We didn't know it would cause that kind of outpouring of emotion."

Four decades after they first sang it for their publisher, Noel and Gloria have heard hundreds of different versions of their song. While each is special in its own way, Gloria explained that it was Robert Goulet's that made even the songwriters step back and listen:

"When Robert Goulet came to the line, 'Pray for peace people everywhere,' he almost shouted those words out. It was so powerful!"

Goulet had gotten it right. That shout was exactly what Noel thought the whole world needed to be doing each day— *demanding* peace for all people everywhere.

The hands of the woman who composed the music have now been silenced by an operation that keeps her from playing the piano. Noel, whose past experiences brought the words to life, recently had a stroke; he can no longer speak, much less sing. Yet thanks to the song that brought both Gloria and Noel to the spotlight, the message of peace on earth and goodwill toward all found in "Do You Hear What I Hear?" touches millions each year.

THE FIRST NOEL

"The First Noel" is one of the oldest Christmas ballads still sung today. Though it first appeared in print in 1833, the song goes back at least three hundred years prior to that. The exact place and time of its origin are in doubt, with both France and England claiming it as a part of their heritage. The spelling of *noel* would seem to indicate a French connection, though there seems to be more evidence pointing to this carol migrating from Britain to France rather than the other way around. What cannot be doubted is the faith and spirit of the song's writer; his Christian witness comes alive each time the old carol is sung!

Just as there are two different points of view as to where this carol was first written, there are also two different ways of spelling the song's title. In England, and sometimes in America, the spelling of *noel* is altered and the old carol is known as "The First Nowell." In France it is always spelled "Noel." What *noel* or *nowell* means in both languages is the same—a joyful shout expressing the exhilaration at the birth of Christ. Yet while the song's anonymous writer obviously knew enough about language to use this all-encompassing term to begin the chorus, he wildly missed the mark on several scriptural points in this song. This gives us additional insight into the background of the inspired voice behind the carol.

"The First Noel" is one of the few surviving early Christmas standards that can genuinely be earmarked as a folk song. Whoever was responsible for writing this carol was obviously incredibly enthusiastic about Christmas and fully understood the wonder of Christ's birth, but didn't have a full grasp on the Scriptures that told the story of that birth. During the Middle Ages, this was often the rule rather than the exception.

When "The First Noel" was written, there were very few Bibles in circulation. Most were either in churches or monasteries and were written in Latin. Common people rarely saw a Bible in person, and even if they would have, they probably wouldn't have been able to read the words in the sacred book, since most people living in those times were illiterate

This was probably the case with the composer of "The First Noel." With no ready Bible to guide him, the writer drew from the stories he had been told about the events of Christ's birth. Most he recounted accurately, but he erred when he depicted the shepherds following the star to Christ's birthplace. The Bible does not mention the star with the shepherds, only with the wise men.

Another key element of this old hymn—the way in which the sentences are structured—indicates that it was written by a man with no formal language training. Phrasing in the original lyrics, such as "This child truly there born he was," is simply not the way a learned hymn writer such as Wesley or Murray would have written. Nevertheless, the spirit found in "The First Noel" more than makes up for its lack of professional

The first noel the angel did say
Was to certain poor shepherds
    in fields as they lay —
In fields where they lay keeping
    their sheep,
On a cold winter's night that
    was so deep.

Chorus:
Noel, noel, noel, noel,
Born is the King of Israel.

They looked up and saw a star
Shining in the east, beyond
    them far;
And to the earth it gave great
    light,
And so it continued both day
    and night.

Chorus

And by the light of that same
    star,
Three wise men came from
    country far;

To seek for a king was their
    intent,
And to follow the star wherever
    it went.

Chorus

This star drew nigh to the
    northwest,
O'er Bethlehem it took its rest;
And there it did both stop and
    stay,
Right over the place where Jesus
    lay.

Chorus

Then entered in those wise men
    three,
Full rev'rently upon their knee;
And offered there, in His pres-
    ence,
Their gold, and myrrh, and
    frankincense.

Chorus

markers. That spirit, coupled with an annual Scandinavian event, probably guaranteed the survival of the old carol.

During the Middle Ages, English peasants had adopted the Viking custom of the Yule log. Each winter a family would go out into the woods, cut down a huge tree, drag it back home, cut away its branches, and hollow out its core. They then filled the hole with oils, spices, and other sweet-smelling ingredients, and set the log in the fireplace. Kindling was sprinkled around the Yule log, and a daughter or a wife would light the fire with a splinter left over from last year's log. Families that burned a Yule log each year believed that good luck would befall their household.

When those who embraced this custom became Christians, they adapted the Yule log to Christmas. Eventually the timber came to symbolize the wood of the cross, and the sweet packing to represent the beautiful life Christ offered each Christian— His ultimate sacrifice on that cross. The log was brought into the home on Christmas Eve and was lit. It was hoped that the log would burn for the entire twelve days of Christmas, its embers dying January 6, the day the wise men arrived with their gifts for Jesus. If the log lasted that long, it was a sign that the household was blessed.

In England, "The First Noel" was sung each year by many peasants as they lit the Yule log. Therefore, this became the song that started the entire Christmas season. Especially for children, this carol meant the beginning of the most wonderful time of the year. Down through the ages, the tradition of the Yule log carried with it the music of this folk carol. Though its words and music were not written down, "The First Noel" survived.

For the first three hundred years of its existence, "The First Noel," like all other carols, was not a part of religious services. New songs, even if they embraced a story from the Scriptures, were not allowed in most churches. Because the clergy disdained carols like "The First Noel," these songs truly became the holiday voice of the people. They related the joy of Christmas, the wonder of God sending a Son to save every man and woman, no matter their station in life. The songs became part of family tradition. Many of the holidays' most beloved songs would have been lost if common folks had not passed them down from generation to generation.

Both "The First Noel" and the Christmas Yule log tradition found their way to France around the fifteenth century. Supposedly the song was introduced to the French people by British minstrels. Like the English, the common people of France embraced the music and the message. They also gave it their own twist: Children in this country often sang this carol as a round.

"The First Noel" finally was published by William Sandys in 1833. A lawyer by trade, Sandys loved music and spent his spare time collecting both French and English folk songs. In his book on Christmas folk songs he included "The First Noel." Already a favorite with the peasant class, by the mid–1800s, when the Church of England began to use new songs during services, "The First Noel" found universal acclaim.

Today this song, obviously inspired by the story of the birth of a Savior and probably written by a common, illiterate man, remains one of the most loved carols of all time. Still, one must wonder why "The First Noel" has survived while thousands of other folk songs about Christmas—many of them better written— have been forgotten. Most likely because the writer brought a rare, jubilant spirit to the song. Anyone who has sung "The First Noel" would have no doubt that the composer not only believed every word he wrote but was excited about the story he was sharing. "The First Noel," therefore, represents the real essence of Christmas, the one element that eludes so many during each holiday season: the announcement of Christ's arrival on earth. While the tradition of the Yule log has all but died out, the message of "The First Noel" still burns brightly.

GO TELL IT ON THE MOUNTAIN

The contribution of unknown African American slaves to Christian music is remarkable. As a largely uneducated people, longing for freedom, suffering incredible cruelty and humiliation, many still somehow managed to encounter the powerful touch of the Holy Spirit in ways that manifested themselves in songs of unparalleled majesty and beauty.

Even more amazing than the songs themselves is the fact that any survived at all. Many of these composers of spirituals could not read or write. For the most part, their works were unpublished for decades and passed along only in the oral tradition. A few songs were spread from the fields to small slave churches along roads via work gangs, and eventually to white churches and even large concert halls in both the South and North. Many, however, were lost, their inspirational lessons in song forgotten, as were the testimonies they contained. Perhaps all of them would have been gone

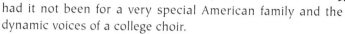

had it not been for a very special American family and the dynamic voices of a college choir.

Not long after the Civil War, a man named John Wesley Work was an African American church choir director in Nashville, Tennessee. A scholar as well as a musician, Work had a deep interest in music that defined the experience of the Negro in America. One of the few educated African Americans in the South, Work felt the new generation of black southerners might best understand the importance of spirituality by learning the songs their ancestors sang during the days of slavery.

In Work's choir were several members of the Fisk Jubilee Singers from the nearby black college of the same name. As Work influenced the Jubilee Singers with his thoughts and music, the singers would pass that influence to the world through their uplifting arrangements of Negro spirituals. During an era when few Negroes were able to travel more than a few miles from their birthplace, the Fisk Jubilee Singers toured the world, appearing in England before Queen Victoria and at the White House in front of President Chester Arthur. Their music revealed a passion for life and living that few people had ever experienced, and they became a monumental force in first exposing the musical talents of African Americans.

John Work passed his love of music and history onto his son, John Wesley Work II. The latter became a folk singer, composer, and collector of Negro spirituals, and, eventually, a professor of history and Latin at Fisk College. His wife was the music teacher for the Jubilee Singers. Along with Work's brother, Frederick, this second generation of Works kept the flame of spiritual music burning brightly and saved a huge number of Negro folk songs from being lost or forgotten.

There will always be some debate over who first uncovered the song "Go Tell It on the Mountain," but Frederick Work was

When I was a seeker
I sought both night and day,
I asked the Lord to help me,
And he showed me the way.

Chorus:
Go tell it on the mountain,
Over the hills and everywhere,
Go tell it on the mountain,
Our Jesus Christ is born.

He made me a watchman
Upon a city wall,
And if I am a Christian,
I am the least of all.

Chorus

When I was a seeker
I sought both night and day,
I asked the Lord to help me,
And he showed me the way.

Chorus

one of the first to note the song's power and potential. The song had come from the fields of the South, born from the inspiration of a slave's Christmas, and it was unique in that, of the hundreds of Negro spirituals the Work family saved from extinction, few had been written about Christmas. Most, as would seem only natural, centered on earthly pain and suffering, and the joy and happiness that only heaven seemed to offer. Yet here, standing against the backdrop of such haunting spirituals as "Sometimes I Feel Like a Motherless Child," was "Go Tell It on the Mountain," a triumphant piece that embraced the wonder of lowly shepherds touched by God at the very first Christmas.

John II and Frederick studied the words and the basic melody to "Go Tell It on the Mountain." Not wanting to change the dramatic impact of the song's lyrics, they left them intact, but the brothers did rearrange the music into an anthem-like structure that would suit choirs such as the Fisk Jubilee Singers. Beginning in the 1880s, that group took the song to the world.

As the Fisk Jubilee Singers introduced the song to the people throughout this country and beyond, many compared the melody to two other Civil War songs, "We'll March Around Jerusalem" and "Tramp, Tramp, Tramp, the Boys are Marching." The Work brothers might have been influenced by both of these folk songs, but neither of them could come close to the message and the power of the words that sprang from a lowly slave's heart. With no hope of earthly freedom, probably unable to even read the Bible, this unknown slave imagined the emotions of shepherds as a powerful light from heaven shone down on them. Frightened by a power they couldn't begin to understand, they were greeted by angelic voices trumpeting the birth of a Savior. Leaving their flock, not fully understanding why they were going, these confused men went to see a baby in the most humble of surroundings. And in that place, these shepherds found understanding, knowledge, and love. As crowds listened to the choir from Fisk perform the song, many were brought to tears, others to their knees.

In 1909, "Go Tell It on the Mountain" was published in Thomas P. Fenner's book *Religious Folk Songs of the Negro as Sung on the Plantations.* Still, without the continued contribution of a third generation of the Work family, this song, and scores of other spirituals, would probably have faded away forever.

Like his father and grandfather, John Work III, a graduate of Julliard, was a devoted student of history and music. Embracing his family's passion, this third-generation member of the Work family continued to uncover and save unknown spirituals, many times traveling hundreds of miles to seek out elderly slaves who had sung them in the fields. John Work III devoted years of his life documenting this important facet of American culture.

In the midst of the Great Depression, Work took another look at what his uncle and father had done with "Go Tell It on the

Mountain." Using their notes and arrangements as well as the materials he had dug up through interviews and research, he took the old song and reworked it one more time, adding a new arrangement and at least one new stanza. It is unknown if Work composed these new lyrics or simply found them during his research, but they fit perfectly with the words the Fisk Jubilee Singers had sung fifty years before. John Work III's arrangement—the one we know today—was published in *American Negro Songs and Spirituals* in 1940.

Over the past fifty years, the popularity of "Go Tell It on the Mountain" has continued to grow. The song's melody is infectious, but it is the spirit of the words that seem to provide the song's real power. As an unknown slave revealed his own prayers and faith, he had little knowledge that the inspiration he felt—probably the only thing of value he ever possessed— would eventually touch millions around the world. Truly, this humble man did not tell the news only on the mountain, but "over the hills and everywhere."

God Rest Ye Merry Gentlemen

*O*ddly enough, understanding the original meaning behind this song—one of the most misunderstood carols of Christmas—also helps explain one of the most misused words describing Christmas itself. What Americans hear when they listen to "God Rest Ye Merry Gentlemen" is not anything like what the English peasants meant when they first sang this song more than five hundred years ago. Because of how wonderfully it tells the Christmas story, the song earned a prominent spot in Dickens's classic novel *A Christmas Carol.* If people today fully understood its unique lyrics, most would probably designate "God Rest Ye Merry Gentlemen" as one of the most profound and meaningful hymns in the world.

Like so many early Christmas songs, this carol was written as a direct reaction to the music of the fifteenth-century church. During this period, songs used by organized religion for worship were usually written in Latin and had dark, somber melodies, offering singers and listeners little inspiration or joy.

In fact, though few admitted it in public, most church members secretly disliked the accepted religious songs of the day. Yet the laymen of the time had no power over the way they worshiped and had to accept things as they were.

So, while they continued to go to worship, commoners created their own church music outside the walls of the cathedrals and chapels. In this way, the peasant class led a quiet rebellion against the tone of current religious music by writing religious folk songs that were light, lively, and penned in common language. These Christmas folk songs became the foundation of what are now known as Christmas carols.

"God Rest Ye Merry Gentlemen" was the most famous and most loved of all the early carols. Written with an upbeat melody and speaking of the birth of Jesus in joyful terms, the song may have shocked early church leaders, but it charmed their flocks. Not only did they sing to this carol, they danced to it.

The lyrics of the song reveal that the unknown writer knew the story of Jesus' birth well. He included the high points of the gospel throughout the carol's verses. The writer also fully understood the power of Christ and what his arrival meant to all who embraced it. In the case of this writer, comprehending the full and personal meaning of the birth of the Son of God brought forth enthusiasm and joy simply not found in any other church songs of the period. Though it might have been rejected by the church leaders, "God Rest Ye Merry Gentlemen" better presented the message of the first Christmas and the life of Jesus than did many of the songs used in formal worship of the day.

The carol was sung for hundreds of years before it was finally published in the nineteenth century. By that time — thanks in part to Queen Victoria's love of such songs — it found favor in the Anglican church. Soon even the protestant English clergy of the Victorian era were enthusiastically teaching "God

God rest ye merry gentlemen,
Let nothing you dismay.
Remember Christ our Savior
Was born on Christmas day,
To save us all from Satan's pow'r
When we were gone astray;

Chorus:
O tidings of comfort and joy,
Comfort and joy,
O tidings of comfort and joy.

From God our heavenly Father
A blessed angel came.
And unto certain shepherds
Brought tidings of the same,
How that in Bethlehem was born
The Son of God by name:

Chorus

"Fear not," then said the angel,
"Let nothing you affright,
This day is born a Savior,
Of virtue, power, and might;
So frequently to vanquish all
The friends of Satan quite;"

Chorus

The shepherds at those tidings
Rejoiced much in mind,
And left their flocks a-feeding,
In tempest, storm, and wind,
And went to Bethlehem straight-
way
This blessed babe to find:

Chorus

But when to Bethlehem they came,
Whereat this infant lay
They found him in a manger,
Where oxen feed on hay;
His mother Mary kneeling,
Unto the Lord did pray:

Chorus

Now to the Lord sing praises,
All you within this place,
And with true love and brother-
hood
Each other now embrace;
This holy tide of Christmas
All others doth deface:

Chorus

Rest Ye Merry Gentlemen" to their parishioners. Crossing the ocean to both Europe and America, the carol became popular throughout the Christian world. It is still sung in much the same way as it was five hundred years ago. The only problem is that, as a result of the evolution of the English language, few of today's singers fully understand the beginning of each of the carol's many verses.

When people today say "Merry Christmas!" the word *merry* means "happy." When "God Rest Ye Merry Gentlemen" was written, *merry* had a very different meaning. Robin Hood's Merry Men might have been happy, but the *merry* that described them meant "great" and "mighty." Thus, in the Middle Ages, a strong army was a merry army, a great singer was a merry singer, and a mighty ruler was a merry ruler.

So when the English carolers of the Victorian era sang the words "merry gentlemen," they meant great or mighty men. *Ye* means "you," but even when translated to "God rest you mighty gentlemen," the song still makes very little sense. This is due to one last word that has a much different meaning in today's world, as well as a lost punctuation mark.

The word *rest* in "God Rest Ye Merry Gentlemen" simply means "keep" or "make." And to completely uncover the final key to solving this mystery of meaning, a comma needs to be placed after the word *merry*. Therefore, in modern English, the first line of "God Rest Ye Merry Gentlemen" should read, "God make you mighty, gentlemen." Using this translation, the old carol suddenly makes perfect sense, as does the most common saying of the holidays, "Merry Christmas!"

You might wonder why, when most don't fully understand the real meaning of "God Rest Ye Merry Gentlemen," the old carol has remained popular. The world's love for this song is probably due to its upbeat melody paired with the telling of the most upbeat story the world has ever known. Those who sing it naturally get caught up in the celebratory mood of the message, embracing the same emotions that those first to visit the baby Jesus must have felt. As the angel told the shepherds, "I bring you good news of great joy." That joy and the power of faith can be felt and experienced in every note and word of "God Rest Ye Merry Gentlemen." You just have to know how to translate the words into the language of the day in order to have a very "Mighty Christmas!"

GOOD CHRISTIAN MEN, REJOICE

One of the most uplifting of the ancient carols, "Good Christian Men, Rejoice" is the product of two men who were persecuted for their religious convictions, endured great personal hardships, suffered through lingering illness, and died in relative obscurity, never accepted by the church they loved. Though both vowed to serve the Lord and take the message of salvation to a lost world, both probably believed they had accomplished little of lasting value as they struggled to follow their call. For Heinrich Suso and John Mason Neale, nothing could have been farther from the truth.

Heinrich Suso was born in 1295, the son of a German nobleman. Educated at the best schools, pampered in luxury, Heinrich was largely insulated from a world where only a precious few did more than endure each passing day. Poverty and disease were everywhere. The aptly named Dark Age was a time of cruelty, prejudice, and despair. A separation of people into social classes meant the very small, elite branch had almost everything and the rest of society had nothing.

Sadly, there was no movement between classes; if you were born without means, you were doomed to live and die that way. And if you were born poor, for every laugh there were a thousand cries.

Suso, who could have risen through his family ranks to a ruling status in his native land, instead chose to be a servant. Accepting a call to the priesthood, he became a Dominican monk. If all he had done was serve in a parish, he would have probably remained unknown. Yet in 1326, the priest felt moved to write the *Little Book of Truth*, a vibrant defense of progressive thinking in the church. In his work, Suso justified taking the gospel and opening it in a way that would bring hope, compassion, and understanding to the common people. But instead of being held up as a man who truly understood the message that Jesus had brought to the earth, the priest was tried for heresy.

Rather than still his voice, Suso felt a call to continue what he saw as a divine war. A year later, the unrepentant monk continued his battle with figures of authority by penning the *Little Book of Eternal Wisdom*. Unlike most religious books of the time, this one was essentially a practical work written in simple language. It wasn't for clerics or professors, it was for the common people. This was a radical concept. Who would dare think that simple people would have any interest in understanding God and the message he brought to the world in the form of Christ?

Unable to control the priest and afraid that his radical thinking might cause a revolt, in 1329 the Pope condemned Suso. Eventually the German king exiled him. Suso fled to Switzerland. For a man born of noble blood, exile was the ultimate humiliation. Over the course of the next few years, the well-meaning priest suffered vicious persecution and slander. Yet even in the face of death threats, he refused to turn his back on the church, his calling, or his desire to share the gospel with the masses.

Wanting to bring joy to the practice of the Christian faith, Suso preached of the happiness he found in walking with God. Many wondered how such a reviled man could find such blessings in life. He explained that God gave him peace and inspiration during every waking hour, and even while he rested. It was during the latter that the priest was given a vehicle to carry his message to the people.

One night, Suso found himself immersed in a dream so real that he became a part of it. In his dream, the priest saw countless angels not only singing, but dancing. He listened as they sang, and eventually joined with them in "an ecstatic dance." When he awoke, he not only remembered the dream in vivid detail, but also recalled the words and the music. Feeling led by divine guidance, Suso picked up a quill and ink and recorded "Good Christian Men, Rejoice" to paper. Until his death in 1366, he continued to reach the common man with this song and its message.

"Good Christian Men, Rejoice" was as radical a hymn as Suso's thinking was progressive. Christian music of that era was usually solemn, based totally on Scripture, and never written in the common language. Suso had broken all three rules. His song embraced the joy of being a believer and enjoined a spirit whose meaning any child could understand. Although it was not immediately accepted by the church itself, the German people quickly and enthusiastically took the song to heart. They believed that just as Suso had been a priest to the common people, his song was a song for them as well.

It would be more than 150 years before the carol inspired by a priest's dream found its way into print, but just because it

Good Christian men, rejoice
With heart, and soul, and voice;
Give ye heed to what we say:
News! News! Jesus Christ is
    born today!
Ox and ass before Him bow,
And He is in the manger now;
Christ is born today!
Christ is born today!

Good Christian men, rejoice
With heart, and soul, and
    voice;
Now ye hear of endless bliss:
Joy! Joy! Jesus Christ was born
    for this!

He hath ope'd the heav'nly
    door,
And man is blessed ever more;
Christ was born for this!
Christ was born for this!

Good Christian men, rejoice
With heart, and soul, and
    voice;
Now ye need not fear the grave:
Peace! Peace! Jesus Christ was
    born to save!
Calls you one and calls you all,
To gain His ever lasting hall;
Christ was born to save!
Christ was born to save!

wasn't published didn't mean that the song didn't inspire other writers in Germany—including Martin Luther—to compose hymns in the common language for the common people. Suso's radical thinking became part of the primary foundation for a revolution in the way most people viewed their relationship with Christ. Even the Catholic church would come to realize that the priest had been right, and in 1831 the Pope canonized Heinrich Suso.

❋

James Mason Neale, a Church of England priest, hymn writer, and scholar whose work included "All Glory, Laud and Honor," was another free thinker impressed with Suso's ideas and song. It is understandable that Neale was deeply moved by the song's attempt to bring the joy of salvation to the common man. In a world filled with sadness, he wanted everyone to know the joy that came when Christ entered a believer's heart. Sadly, in the mid–1800s, Neale's views of an exuberant faith were viewed as radical.

He was exiled to a pastorate far from his native England and  even stoned and beaten by a crowd once for his beliefs. Although ridiculed by the leadership of his own denomination, Neale still sought out ways to reach the lost and forgotten. In a radical move for a priest in the Church of England, and over the objections of his superiors, Neale began an order of women, the Sisterhood of St. Margaret, to feed the poor, take care of orphaned children, and minister to prostitutes. Though this group would touch tens of thousands, it brought death threats to Neale and the women who served in the Sisterhood. Nevertheless, in 1853 an English publisher released Neale's English translation of "Good Christian Men, Rejoice" in *Carols for Christmastide.* This book would pave the way for the song to be taken to the world.

By 1900, "Good Christian Men, Rejoice" had become one of the most popular carols in both America and Europe. A century later, it is still one of the most beloved Christmas songs in the world.

In spite of its popularity, "Good Christian Men, Rejoice" is rarely performed by huge choirs or in the best concert halls and cathedrals. The fact that the classical crowd has largely over-looked this song would probably please Heinrich Suso and John Mason Neale. After all, both men had suffered shame and ridicule because of their efforts to spread the Good News to the very people Christ spoke of during his own life on earth — "the least of these."

GOOD KING WENCESLAS

*O*f all the ancient legends that surround Christmas, the tale about King Wenceslaus (later spelled Wenceslas) stands out. Though the carol was composed by noted songwriter and priest, John Mason Neale, the song is based less on a writer's inspiration than on historical fact. King Wenceslaus was a real member of European royalty, a ruler who daily touched his subjects with Christian kindness and charity. For many in the Dark Ages, this king was the role model for Santa Claus. Today, over a thousand years after his death, King Wenceslaus remains a role model for Christian people everywhere.

The son of Duke Borivoy of Bohemia, Wenceslaus had the good fortune to be raised by his grandmother, Ludmilla. Ludmilla was a devoted Christian woman who taught her grandson the meaning of faith, hope, and charity. Wenceslaus took his grandmother's lessons to heart, and in 922, when Duke Borivoy was killed in battle, the youngster seemed ready to put what he had learned into action. At the tender age of fifteen,

Wenceslaus, just a few minutes older than his twin brother, Boleslaus, was made the leader of Bohemia.

As the young duke attempted to guide the troubled nation, his mother, Drahomira, and his brother, Boleslaus, instituted a pagan revolt. They assassinated Ludmilla as she prayed, then attempted to overthrow Wenceslaus. The teen took charge, put down the rebellion, and in an act of Christian kindness, expelled his mother and brother rather than executing them. The tiny nation was amazed that the boy would react with such great mercy.

With the wisdom of Solomon, the young duke set up a nation built on true justice and mercy. He enacted laws in the manner he thought would best serve his Lord. He even journeyed out into the country seeking insight as to what his people needed. When possible, he shared everything from firewood to meat with his subjects. He took pity on the poor and urged those blessed with wealth to reach out to the less fortunate. In large part due to Wenceslaus's example, a host of pagan peasants turned to Christianity. It was a revival unlike any had ever seen in the country.

When Wenceslaus married and had a son, all of Bohemia celebrated. Peasants and powerful landlords sought the man out, offering their prayers for long life and happiness. With a smile on his face, the leader assured them that he was praying for their happiness as well. In the years that followed, the duke and his subjects continued to share both their prayers and their blessings with one another each day. Rarely had a leader been as universally revered as was Wenceslaus.

And Wenceslaus loved Christmas. Centuries before gift giving became a part of the holiday tradition, the young leader embraced the joy of sharing his bounty with others. Inspired by a sincere spirit of compassion, each Christmas Eve the duke sought out the most needy of his subjects and visited them. With his pages at his side, Wenceslaus brought food, firewood, and clothing. After greeting all in the household, the duke would continue to the next stop. Though often faced with harsh weather conditions, Wenceslaus never postponed his rounds. Like a tenth century Saint Nick, the kindly young man made the night before Christmas special for scores of families. For many, a Christmas Eve visit from the duke was an answered prayer and a special reason to celebrate the birth of Jesus.

In 929, when he was just twenty-two years old, Wenceslaus was on his way to church for his daily prayers. As he greeted his subjects and took time to ask about their health, the warm look on the man's face assured each of them that he cared deeply about their welfare. Smiling and shouting greetings, he continued to the chapel. Just before entering, he heard a familiar voice. Turning, he must have been surprised when his brother greeted him. As a confused look crossed the Duke's face, Boleslaus's confederates ran up to Wenceslaus and stabbed him. Falling to his knees on the church steps, the dying ruler looked up and whispered, "Brother, may God forgive you." Then he died.

It was a group of powerful pagan leaders who had supported Boleslaus's overthrow of Wenceslaus. Amazingly, when the young man realized what he had done, the new duke turned away from his colleagues and embraced the faith that had guided his brother's life and rule. Though he had planned the revolt that had killed his twin, it was Boleslaus who sustained the legend of Wenceslaus. Thanks to the man who killed his brother, the Crown of Wenceslaus became the symbol of the Czech nation.

❋

John Mason Neale closely identified with Wenceslaus in that he, too, reached out to saint and sinner alike. (For more on

Good King Wenceslas looked out,
On the Feast of Stephen,
When the snow lay round about,
Deep and crisp and even;
Brightly shone the moon that
    night,
Tho' the frost was cruel,
When a poor man came in sight,
Gath'ring winter fuel.

"Hither, page, and stand by me,
If thou know'st it, telling,
Yonder peasant, who is he?
Where and what his dwelling?"
"Sire, he lives a good league
    hence,
Underneath the mountain;
Right against the forest fence,
By Saint Agnes' fountain."

"Bring me flesh, and bring me
    wine,
Bring me pine logs hither:
Thou and I will see him dine,
When we bear them thither."

Page and monarch, forth they
    went,
Forth they went together;
Thro' the rude wind's wild lament
And the bitter weather.

"Sire, the night is darker now,
And the wind blows stronger;
Fails my heart, I know not how,
I can go no longer."
"Mark my footsteps, good my
    page;
Tread thou in them boldly:
Thou shalt find the winter's rage
Freeze thy blood less coldly."

In his master's steps he trod
Where the snow lay dinted;
Heat was in the very sod
Which the saint had printed.
Therefore, Christian men, be sure,
Wealth or rank possessing,
Ye who now will bless the poor,
Shall yourselves find blessing.

Neale, see the essay on "Good Christian Men, Rejoice.") Though often rebuked by Christians, Neale constantly tried to reform prostitutes, thieves, and even murderers. Any man or woman who ventured into his path felt the Englishman's loving touch.

When not involved in his mission outreach, Neale spent a great deal of time reviewing ancient Latin songs and text, often translating them into English for use in church services. One of the stories he came across was the biography of Wenceslaus. Sensing that the Duke would make a wonderful role model for children, Neale rewrote the old tale in verse form, making the Duke a King, and matching his lyrics to a Latin melody, "Tempus adest floridum." It now seems ironic that Neale's Christmas carol would be sung to a tune that when translated meant "Spring has unwrapped her flowers." Yet because Wenceslaus brought his poorest subjects a breath of fresh air and warmth to the darkest winter days, perhaps Neale's choice was no accident.

When published, "Good King Wenceslas" quickly became a holiday favorite in Europe. By the last part of the nineteenth century it was sung throughout the United States as well. This carol was largely responsible for making the legend of Wenceslaus known throughout the world, as it touched upon the Bohemian saint's examples of faith, hope, and charity.

Suddenly the symbol of Czech independence became the crown jewel of Christian living.

One of the most telling facets of the Duke's legendary life can be found in the final verse of "Good King Wenceslas." In the carol, the King reminds his page that when a person is alone, life is dark and bleak. But when a person reaches out to others—like Christ reached out to those in need—then that person never walks alone. Christ and those who have been touched by kindness are there to make each step of the journey easier and brighter. Just as the page's walk was made easier by following in the King's footsteps, so the King's way was made easier by following in the steps of Christ.

Wenceslaus and Neale both held positions of importance. Either could have chosen to be served by others, yet each instead devoted their lives to service. Both understood the tenants of faith, hope, and charity and throughout their lives reached out to others with compassion and love. Now the carol "Good King Wenceslas" reminds the world that the spirit of Christmas giving didn't begin with Santa Claus, nor should it end there. It can be alive in all who choose to give with love and live by faith.

HARK! THE HERALD ANGELS SING

*I*n 1847, William Cummings, just sixteen years old, was singing one of the tenor leads in Felix Mendelssohn's opera *Elijah*. For the young tenor, to be directed by one of the most renowned composers in the world was a dream come true. It is little wonder that that night made an indelible impression on Cummings and ultimately gave birth to a marvelous duo of lyric and melody.

Almost three decades before Cummings was born, England's premier Christian poet and songwriter, Charles Wesley, died at the age of seventy. Wesley, the youngest of eighteen children, wrote more than three thousand hymns, many of which—such as "Jesus Christ Is Risen Today" and "Love Divine All Loves Excelling"—are still sung by millions. Yet the life and work of the man still remembered today as one of the greatest hymn writers in history could have been much different. If not for a dispute with an employer, Wesley's contributions to both music and the establishment of a Christian movement might never have happened.

Wesley began his formal education at the Westminster School in 1716. He then studied at Christ College in Oxford. In 1735, at the age of twenty-eight, Charles sailed for Georgia to become secretary to General James Oglethorpe. In short order, Wesley found himself missing his home and family and feeling stifled in his new role. In less than a year he quit his job and returned to London.

Assigned to a church in Islington, England, Wesley immediately began making waves. His outlook was radically different from most other English clergy of the time. He visited prisons, was a strong supporter of individual thinking, often held church services outdoors, and believed Christian music needed to be infused with heavy doses of personal witness, energy, and enthusiasm. He kept his mind sharp through daily Bible study and hours spent writing music.

In 1737, during his daily quiet time, Wesley was working on a new Christmas composition. When the pastor jotted down the line, "Hark! how all the welkin rings, glory to the King of Kings," the new song quickly fell together. *Welkin,* a word foreign to most today, literally means the "vault of heaven makes a long noise." Thus, when heaven sends forth a loud pronouncement, the entire power of the King is revealed. Set to one of the writer's own unique melodies, "Hark! How All The Welkin Rings" premiered in Wesley's own church and quickly gained favor with other congregations following the new Methodist movement. Naturally, the writer was pleased with the acceptance of his work. However, when his old college friend, George Whitefield, finally published the song, Wesley's benevolent pride turned to rage.

Whitefield, a former bartender turned Calvinist preacher, was often at theological odds with Wesley. Wesley might have been pushing for reform, but Whitefield wanted to lead a revolution. After being ordained as a priest in the Church of England, Whitefield's fiery rhetoric and evangelical messages kept him in constant trouble with the church. Because of his militant approach, Whitefield was soon banned from the Anglican churches of his day and forced to mostly preach in privately organized, open-air meetings. From Whitefield's informal meetings sprang the revival movement that would soon explode in the United States.

Though much more charismatic, Whitefield was not as well educated as Wesley and so his interpretation of the Scriptures was a tad more liberal and not so literal. True to form, when Whitefield published Wesley's Christmas song, he changed the words without consulting the writer. When Wesley read the new first line, "Hark! the herald angels sing," he was incensed. Nowhere in the Bible did angels sing about the birth of Christ. Yet because of Whitefield's change in one line, today most people believe that Luke 2:13 refers to singing angels rather than, "A great company of the heavenly host [spiritual beings not normally seen who watch over man] appeared with the angel, praising God and saying, 'Glory to God in the highest, and on earth peace to men on whom his favor rests.'"

As long as he lived, Wesley never sang Whitefield's rework of his song. Yet even if the writer refused to acknowledge the change, millions around the world soon embraced singing angels in sermons, music, literature, and art. One of those was William Cummings.

The same year that Cummings sang for Felix Mendelssohn, the famous composer and conductor died at the young age of thirty-eight. Mendelssohn had been born a Jew, but had adopted the Christian faith as a child. Yet by and large, the composer's music centered on the world, not on his faith. Aside

Hark! the herald angels sing,
"Glory to the newborn King;
Peace on earth, and mercy
    mild —
God and sinners reconciled!"
Joyful, all ye nations, rise,
Join the triumph of the skies;
With th'angelic host proclaim,
"Christ is born in Bethlehem."
Hark! the herald angels sing,
"Glory to the newborn King!"

Christ, by highest heav'n adored,
Christ, the everlasting Lord:
Late in time behold Him come,
Offspring of a virgin's womb.
Veiled in flesh, the God-head see,
Hail th'incarnate Deity!
Pleased as man with men to
    dwell,
Jesus, our Emmanuel!
Hark! the herald angels sing,
"Glory to the newborn King!"

Hail, the heav'n-born Prince of
    Peace!
Hail, the Sun of Righteousness!
Light and life to all He brings,
Ris'n with healing in His wings.
Mild He lays His glory by,
Born that man no more may die;
Born to raise the sons of earth,
Born to give them second birth.
Hark! the herald angels sing,
"Glory to the newborn King!"

Come, Desire of nations, come!
Fix in us Thy humble home:
O, to all Thyself impart,
Formed in each believing heart!
Hark! the herald angels sing,
"Glory to the newborn King!"
Peace on earth, and mercy mild,
God and sinners reconciled!"
Hark! the herald angels sing,
"Glory to the newborn King."

from a work in 1840 that gave a nod toward Johann Gutenberg, the famous Bible printer, and being influenced by Bach, Handel, Mozart, and Beethoven, Mendelssohn's most famous composition was the enduring *Midsummer Night's Dream*.

In 1855, William Cummings combined Mendelssohn's Gutenberg tribute, "Festgesang an die Knustler," with the Whitefield rewrite, "Hark! the Herald Angels Sing." The end result was a dramatic change unimagined by either composer.

Cummings's arrangement of "Hark! the Herald Angels Sing" was first printed in a Methodist hymnal in 1857. Over the next few years it was adopted by other denominations and publishers. Within a decade, the new "Hark! the Herald Angels Sing" was one of the most recognized carols in the world.

The road to acceptance and fame for this Christmas carol began when a misquoted verse of Scripture (Whitefield) was combined with a melody (Cummings) written to honor the man who first printed the Bible (Gutenberg). Although neither Wesley nor Mendelssohn would probably have approved of *this* combination of lyric and melody, it now seems appropriate that the words of a man who lived to evangelize the world for Christ (Wesley) should be tied to a tribute written for a man who invented a method of mass-producing God's Word for all to read.

HAVE YOURSELF A MERRY LITTLE CHRISTMAS

During Hollywood's Golden Era, the movie studios kept the songwriting team of Hugh Martin and Ralph Blane busy. The men worked together and separately on such classic musicals as *Girl Crazy*, *Broadway Rhythm*, and *Gentlemen Prefer Blondes*, as well as scores of other successful presentations. The men also wrote tunes for Broadway and radio that were sung by the likes of Lucille Ball, June Allyson, Lena Horne, Ethel Merman, Mickey Rooney, and Ann Miller. Even though they won many awards and were responsible for millions of record sales, these Hall of Fame writers penned their most beloved hit when MGM asked them to write the music for *Meet Me in St. Louis*. Yet it would take the insight and help of an entertainment legend to put the finishing touches on what would become a timeless holiday offering.

Filmed toward the end of World War II, *Meet Me in St. Louis* starred some of the brightest names at MGM. Mary Astor, Leon Ames, June Lockhart, and Margaret O'Brien were all on the bill and helped make this motion picture one of the finest musicals ever produced. But the movie ultimately belonged to a twenty-two-year-old screen veteran who, five years before, had charmed everyone as Dorothy in *The Wizard of Oz*.

While she was one of Hollywood's top box office draws, Judy Garland needed a strong film to help her overcome the juvenile image created by her role in *The Wizard of Oz* and a long line of teen musicals that had teamed her with Mickey Rooney. To be recognized as a serious actress, she had to have a part that would allow her to shift from child star to legitimate adult lead. *Meet Me in St. Louis* provided the vehicle Garland needed to take her career over the rainbow and onto solid ground. It was Judy's own instincts and sincere voice that made one moment in the film an unforgettable holiday gift that still touches people today.

For one of the film's key scenes, Judy's character, Esther, was to sing a song to her sad little sister, Tootie. The younger girl was worried that when her family moved to New York from Missouri, Santa would not be able to find her. Esther was concerned as well, but not about Saint Nick. She had just fallen in love and realized the family's move would end her cherished relationship before it really got started. Though the scene was set on a beautiful Christmas Eve night, both sisters felt they were facing the end of the world.

Looking out over a snow-covered lawn from an upstairs window, Judy's character wound a music box and began to sing. The songwriters felt that to make the most of the film's suddenly tender and sad atmosphere, they needed a song that was full of irony and pain. So at the beginning of the song, the men penned, "Have yourself a merry little Christmas; it may be your last; next year we will be living in the past."

Thinking they had written a perfect song for this touching and tragic moment in the film, Blane and Martin were probably shocked when Garland refused to sing their "Have Yourself a Merry Little Christmas." She sent the song back to the writers demanding that they put a more positive spin on the number. Judy's desires were backed by the film's director and her future husband, Vincente Minnelli. Unable to convince either of those powers that their instincts were right, Blane and Martin went back to work.

Even though Blane and Martin had guessed right about the needs of the movie, Garland had a better instinct for what the country needed at that moment in history. During much of the past three years Judy had spent every spare moment entertaining American troops. She had visited with the young men, sung for them, and read the fan mail they had written to her. She knew that most of them were young men her age who had spent years fighting for their lives, defending a nation. What these men wanted—more than anything else—was to somehow live through the war and come back home. They wanted, *needed* to believe that there was a lot of life left in front of them.

As she entertained the G.I.s, Garland discovered that her biggest hit, "Somewhere Over the Rainbow," had a much deeper meaning for the men than it did for the casual listener. For millions on the battle lines, "over the rainbow" meant coming home. Judy felt the new Christmas song that would be a part of *Meet Me in St. Louis* needed to bring the same kind of hope as "Somewhere Over the Rainbow" did.

By request, Blane and Martin obligingly wrote a far more upbeat, new opening. There was an obvious encouraging tone in "let your heart be light; from now on our troubles will be out of sight" that presented the kind of message Garland felt America needed. Judy embraced the revised "Have Yourself a Merry Little Christmas" with a passion and emotion that few could understand. This wasn't just another song to Garland; it was a prayer for the millions wanting nothing more than to be home for Christmas. In the new version of "Have Yourself a Merry Little Christmas," listeners in the U.S. and overseas could believe that the war was almost over, that families would be reuniting, and that the promised joy that had been a part of Christmases past would soon be here again.

As moving as Judy's performance of the song in the film was, the Decca single that was released for Christmas 1944 was just as touching. Garland's rich voice revealed the full range of emotions found in the song's lyrics. In an era when Christmas songs seemed to mean more than they ever had before, "Have Yourself a Merry Little Christmas" was one of the best. When Judy sang it to soldiers at the Hollywood Canteen, there wasn't a dry eye in the place. When battle weary men in Europe and the Pacific heard it, they clung to the song as if their dreams were carried on each word and note.

For the next twenty-five years of her often troubled life, Judy Garland seemed to always come alive during Christmas. The holidays somehow renewed the star. It was almost as if singing her signature Christmas standard gave her the gift of new vision and hope, just as the song did for millions of others who felt lonely and sad during the holiday season.

They say that timing is everything. If the original version of "Have Yourself a Merry Little Christmas" would have worked in *Meet Me in St. Louis,* it probably wouldn't have jumped off the screen and taken on a life of its own. But thanks to the instincts of Judy Garland, the song became far more than a moment in a film; it became a timeless, emotional statement about what we all want to have each year, a very merry little Christmas and hope for tomorrow.

I HEARD THE BELLS
ON CHRISTMAS DAY

*M*any view Henry Wadsworth Longfellow as America's greatest poet. Today, 120 years after his death, he is still a giant in literature, and many consider his work inspiring and uplifting. Yet when he wrote, "Believe me, every man has his secret sorrows, which the world knows not; and oftentimes we call a man cold, when he is only sad," Longfellow was surely writing from his own experiences. He knew what it was like to be down and forlorn.

During the nineteenth century—a time when many Americans were first-generation immigrants—Longfellow's family had already been on American shores for several generations. The first Longfellow came to America from Yorkshire, England, in 1676. Among Henry's fabled ancestors were John and Priscilla Alden, as well as an uncle who was a colonial general in the Revolutionary War. Henry was the son of well-known New England lawyer Stephen Longfellow. Born in 1807 in the picturesque seaport of Portland, Maine, the boy first went to school at the age of three. By six, he was already reading classical literature and writing stories. At the tender age of nineteen, the college graduate was given the position of professor of modern language at Bowdoin College. In this role, he not only taught during school terms but also traveled and studied in Europe.

A man of the world by twenty-two, Longfellow wrote his own textbooks. Married in 1831, by 1834 Henry was already viewed as one of his country's most respected scholars. It was hardly a surprise when Harvard wooed him away from Bowdoin. With a wonderful wife, a dynamic reputation, and a fine house overlooking the Charles River, Henry seemed to have it all. Yet, tragically, within a year of his move to Massachusetts, his wife became ill and died.

In an effort to deal with his grief, a mournful Longfellow poured himself into his teaching. It took seven years before he recovered enough from his loss to remarry. With a new love as his foundation, the good life returned to the scholar. One after another, the Longfellows welcomed five children into their home. During this happy period Longfellow wrote such classic poems as "Evangeline," "The Song of Hiawatha," and "The Courtship of Miles Standish." By 1860 he had found wealth and worldwide fame, lionized as one of the greatest writers ever produced by the New World.

However, at the very moment when Henry should have been celebrating the joys brought by his talents, financial security, and stature, tragedy again struck. In spite of being given honorary degrees at Oxford and Cambridge, and an invitation to Windsor by Queen Victoria, 1861 was a year filled with great sadness. While lighting a match, Longfellow's second wife's clothes caught fire and she burned to death. Then, even before he could regain his stride, his faith was again challenged by the American Civil War.

I heard the bells on Christmas
   day
Their old familiar carols play,
And wild and sweet the words
   repeat
Of peace on earth, goodwill to
   men.

I thought how, as the day had
   come,
The belfries of all Christendom
Had rolled along th'unbroken
   song
Of peace on earth, goodwill to
   men.

And in despair I bowed my head:
"There is no peace on earth," I
   said,
"For hate is strong and mocks
   the song
Of peace on earth, goodwill to
   men."

Then from each black, accursed
   mouth
The cannon thundered in the
   South,

And with the sound the carols
   drowned
Of peace on earth, goodwill to
   men.

It was as if an earthquake rent
The hearth-stones of a continent,
And made forlorn, the house-
   holds born
Of peace on earth, goodwill to
   men.

Then pealed the bells more loud
   and deep:
"God is not dead, nor doth He
   sleep;
The wrong shall fail, the right
   prevail,
With peace on earth, goodwill
   to men."

Till ringing, singing on its way
The world revolved from night
   to day —
A voice, a chime, a chant sublime
Of peace on earth, goodwill to
   men!

Longfellow hated the Civil War. It tore at the very fiber of his being to see the United States of America—a nation his family had fought to create and help build—divided by the greed and sinful nature of man. An ardent believer in the power of God to move on earth, the poet all but pleaded with his Lord to end the madness of the war. When his oldest son, nineteen-year-old Charles, was wounded in battle and sent home to recover, the poet's prayers turned to rage.

As Henry tended his son's injuries, saw other wounded soldiers on Cambridge's streets, and visited with families who had lost sons in battle, he asked his friends and his God, "Where is the peace?" Then, picking up his pen and paper, he tried to answer that haunting question.

It was the ringing of Christmas bells that probably inspired the cadence found in his writing on December 25, 1863. That day Longfellow hung his whole message on the tolling of the church bells. Yet while most Christmas verse is light and uplifting, America's greatest poet set his lyrical ode in tones that were largely dark and solemn.

In the original seven stanzas of "I Heard the Bells on Christmas Day," Longfellow focused on Christmas during the Civil War. In his lines one can easily sense the writer's views of slav-

ery and secession; his words divide the war into an effort of God's love and understanding against the devil's hate and anger. It would have been a poem completely void of hope, a testament to the power of Satan, if Henry hadn't finished his work with two verses that embraced the thought, "God is not dead, nor doth He sleep. The wrong shall fail, the right prevail, with peace on earth, goodwill to men." This was a poem that would inspire not only the Union, but soon the whole world.

❋

Almost ten years later, in 1872, an Englishman named John Baptiste Calkin decided to marry music to Longfellow's Christmas poem. The organist and music teacher wrote a soaring melody that contained the power to not only convey the bleak imagery of Longfellow's sadness in the poem's tormented first few verses, but the poet's deep and abiding faith in the ode's exhilarating conclusion. When published, this combination of British music and American lyrics quickly made "I Heard the Bells on Christmas Day" one of the most popular carols in both Europe and the United States. Except for the deletion of the two verses that dwelled on the poet's view of the Civil War, the song remains the same today as it was when first published.

While it has been arranged in anthem form for numerous choirs and recorded countless times by a wide variety of artists, "I Heard the Bells on Christmas Day" is still a very personal song. With its plea for sanity in a world often gone insane, with its hope that somehow the joy, comfort, and peace that Christ was born to offer would be realized, the song has been a musical anchor for millions during the dark days of World War I, World War II, Korea, and Vietnam. Even today, when conflicts and turmoil rule so many different lives, millions still ask where peace and goodwill reside. The answer is one that Longfellow not only knew, but also shared, in his most beloved work.

I WONDER AS I WANDER

*T*he discovery of this Christmas folk song fits well with the ballad's title. For years, John Jacob Niles wandered around the Appalachian Mountains in search of the origins of songs. A composer and singer, Niles was born in Louisville, Kentucky, on April 28, 1892. Inspired by an old black field-worker who sang spirituals learned in his youth, at twenty-five Niles penned his first folk song, "Go 'Way from My Window." That initial offering and its positive reception inspired the young man's passion for folk music, a passion that would eventually become Niles's life's quest.

The real world kept Niles from that quest for some time. To make ends meet, John worked for an adding machine company, then served as a pilot during World War I. It was during his days in Europe that he first put together an impressive catalog of American folk songs. Begging every soldier he met to share a song, Niles wrote down the lyrics and memorized the music of each one. After the war, armed with a suitcase filled with folk music, Niles returned home and continued his education at the Cincinnati Conservatory. When he graduated he moved to Chicago, where he sang with the Lyric Opera and performed on Westinghouse Radio.

In 1925 Niles moved to New York, where he not only sang on radio and stage, but also began to publish music collections of both his original songs and the folk songs he had gathered during the war. By 1940 he was a recording artist on the RCA label and was recognized as one of the nation's top opera singers. His two most successful original works were "Black is the Color of My True Love's Hair" and "Jesus, Jesus, Rest Your Head." Money and fame had made Niles the toast of New York. Yet even as he received standing ovations for singing the best in classical music in front of crowds, dressed in the finest clothing, backstage the man sang folk ditties. There was something about simple American music that just wouldn't leave him alone.

Deciding he was more historian than performer, Niles moved home to Kentucky. With the advent of radio and the automobile, rural music and the traditions that went with it were quickly fading. So in his beloved Appalachian Mountains, Niles spent a good portion of the remainder of his life traveling from town to town, looking for undiscovered folk songs. The library of work he uncovered is one of the most important in music history. One song in particular would become a monument to Niles's years of hard work and a testament to the power of inspired creativity.

On a cold December day in North Carolina, Niles observed people from a poor community going about their daily lives. From his own experience, Niles knew that just a few hundred miles away in New York, people crowded the gaily decorated city streets, stores could not hold all the eager shoppers armed with lists, and holiday music blared from long rows of loud-speakers. Yet in this village he could hear the sound of snow crunching under feet and spy children in ragged clothes looking longingly into windows where a few small toys were displayed. It was as if the modern world had never found this unspoiled place.

While Niles took in the pastoral scene that surrounded him, a solitary voice beckoned ever so faintly. Searching the street, his eyes honed in on a small girl sitting by herself on a bench. Unaware she had an audience, the child was softly singing a song Niles had never heard.

When she finished, the curious songwriter reached into his pocket and pulled out a pencil and tablet. Approaching the little girl, he introduced himself, sat down and then asked about the song. All she knew about it was that her mother had taught it to her, like her grandma had taught it to her mother before her. When asked to sing it again, the red-cheeked youngster smiled and quietly repeated the ballad's short verses.

The song, which the girl called "I Wonder as I Wander," haunted Niles. Long after the child disappeared into the evening, the man continued to study the words. They were unlike any he had ever uncovered in his long search for folk music. Deeply spiritual, incredibly thoughtful, yet obviously composed by someone of little means and education, the lyrics embraced the joy and wonder of Christmas but also lingered on the sacrifice of a child grown into a man that died on a cross. The soaring happiness, combined with unparalleled sorrow, seemed to share the elements of Negro spirituals with the irony of Irish ballads. Both the words and music were perfect, simple, direct, and inspired. Even a master songwriter like Niles couldn't imagine improving on them. *"Where did it come from?"* he wondered as he returned home.

I wonder as I wander out under the sky,
How Jesus the Savior did come for to die.
For poor on'ry people like you and like I. . .
I wonder as I wander out under the sky.

When Mary birthed Jesus 'twas in a cow's stall,
With wise men and farmers and shepherds and all.
But high from God's heaven a star's light did fall,
And the promise of ages it then did recall.

If Jesus had wanted for any wee thing,
A star in the sky, or a bird on the wing,
Or all of God's angels in heav'n for to sing,
He surely could have it, 'cause he was the King.

When Niles brought the song to prominence just before the beginning of World War II, he tried to capture the spirit of the child who had first shared the song with him. Even as he awed audiences with his discovery, the humble singer recognized that his version was not nearly as powerful as the original.

For years, Niles sang "I Wonder as I Wander" and continued to dig into the mystery of the unrecognized genius who composed the carol. It was a quest he pursued until his death in 1980. Yet he could never trace the song back farther than the girl in North Carolina, a child he never found again. It was as if the little one had been an angel sent to deliver a message, a message that embraced the wonder of the Savior's birth and sacrifice. Because of a chance meeting between an unknown child and a man who spent his life wandering America in search of music, the world gained an unforgettable Christmas ballad that has never ceased to cause those who hear it to wonder.

I'LL BE HOME FOR CHRISTMAS

*M*illions of those who once embraced this song—who reverently listened to each word and note and hung on every sentimental thought woven into the lyrics—are now gone. Age has taken a mighty toll on the men and women who first clung to "I'll Be Home for Christmas" as not just a song, but also as a prayer. For young and old during the darkest days of World War II, for sons and daughters, fathers and mothers, grandmothers and grandfathers, aunts and uncles, "I'll Be Home for Christmas" represented their hopes, dreams, and prayers better than any other song, movie, or story. Many who hear this carol today may think it overly maudlin, but when it was released, it quickly became the most powerful song on the hit parade.

The song may very well be one of the simplest Christmas carols ever written. There is an introduction, a single verse and a chorus, just twelve lines that innocently depict a person's longing for home. Yet the way these dozen lines moved a nation during the uncertain times of war, as well as the way

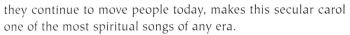
they continue to move people today, makes this secular carol one of the most spiritual songs of any era.

It was 1942, and lyricist Kim Gannon knew the emotional toll of fighting a war on two fronts. In Brooklyn, the writer's home, not only had thousands of families given up their sons to the armed forces, but many had already lost their children in battle. Christmas, traditionally a time of great joy in Gannon's New York borough, felt strangely different that year. The streets were decorated, trees were sold on corner lots, and Santas still rang their bells and smiled at children, but the war had cast a pall over the holidays. It was hard to think of presents or peace on earth when parents anxiously read the news and prayed that every telegraph delivery man would pass them by. To make it all worse, no one was completely sure that the United States and its allies could even win the horrible war.

Kim saw the same gut-wrenching scenes play out every day—the prayers of frantic parents, the tears of newly enlisted soldiers saying their good-byes at train stations, the rush toward mailmen who might carry a letter from a loved one. The writer knew well that the news on the radio was both a curse and a blessing. Everyone felt the need to learn what was going on in the Pacific and Europe, but fear came with that knowledge as well . . . a biting fear when a parent or wife heard that a major battle had broken out in the same place a son, father, or husband had mentioned in their last letter home. With the coming of Christmas, the depression of being separated from loved ones was even worse.

Not only were families of overseas soldiers caught in a world of uncertainty and dread, so were many displaced rural men and women who had moved to New York and other large cities to work in plants and offices. Like many of the men in uniform, the war had taken civilians away from home. Most were spending a Christmas away from family for the very first time, and were lonely and homesick.

When Gannon sat down with pen in hand to capture the unsettling scenes that surrounded her and everyone else in America, the cascade of emotions must have made writing "I'll Be Home for Christmas" very difficult. There was so much to say, so much that would be missed by those split apart by the hellish nightmare of war. Yet rather than try to cover everything, the writer simply wrote, in a straightforward, uncomplicated manner, about the heartache of being away from home at Christmas. Short, direct, and sweet, the poem Kim produced in so few lines somehow completely captured the emotions of hundreds of millions.

Gannon's words were brought to tunesmith Walter Kent. Also a New Yorker, Kent understood the sadness of the holiday season. Kent, who had already composed the sentimental hit "White Cliffs of Dover," inherently knew what the song needed. In his mind's eye, he saw empty chairs at the table, mothers trying to smile through tears as they baked cookies for remaining family members, and unopened presents on the tree. (During this period Christmas presents were often very simple and tied to the tree rather than wrapped and placed under it.) With these pictures

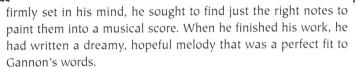

firmly set in his mind, he sought to find just the right notes to paint them into a musical score. When he finished his work, he had written a dreamy, hopeful melody that was a perfect fit to Gannon's words.

One of the true wonders of this song is that it sounds more like a letter home than a typical Christmas carol. Not only is there a real sadness evident in the words and melody, but a hopefulness as well. It's as if the singer were a homesick marine, soldier, or sailor assuring those who missed him that he would soon be there with them again. Ultimately, "I'll Be Home For Christmas" left the listener with the final and urgent plea, "Don't give up, we'll be together soon."

The spiritual nature of this song comes from its almost prayer-like message. Christmas in America had always been about family and remembering the One who started it all. Yet World War II had broken those bonds and disturbed the traditions of the holidays. "I'll Be Home for Christmas" eloquently acknowledged the hope that while things changed, given time, everyone would be home again.

On October 4, 1943, Bing Crosby recorded "I'll Be Home For Christmas." It became his 209th charting single and a follow-up to his holiday hit of 1942, "White Christmas." The latter had stayed on the charts for seventeen weeks during its initial release and reentered the hit parade in 1943 and stayed on there for another month and a half. Yet in the midst of the war, "I'll Be Home for Christmas" received more airplay and generated more sales than did the Crosby hit of the previous year. It quickly became the most requested song at Christmas U.S.O. shows in both Europe and the Pacific. Some historians have said that for service personnel and their families the only inspirational patriotic song that was its equal was "God Bless America."

Throughout World War II, Korea, and Vietnam, the song symbolized and captured the emotions of those on the battle-fronts, as well as the emotions of those back home praying for their safe return. Recorded countless times by scores of different artists, it has sold millions of records. But beyond its remarkable sales is the way the song has been embraced by every facet of society. As a testament to its hopeful nature, even though it does not have a single reference to Jesus or the first Christmas, over the past fifty years it has been used in hundreds of cantatas and church programs.

Today, more than five decades after it was embraced as a World War II holiday prayer, "I'll Be Home for Christmas" stirs new emotions. Most of those who returned home for Christmas after the war have left this world for the next. Yet because of the contributions and sacrifices of the men and women who served our country during those dark days, they will always be home for Christmas in our hearts, memories, and dreams.

IT CAME UPON
THE MIDNIGHT CLEAR

*I*n 1849, a Unitarian minister from Wayland, Massachusetts, was writing a Christmas Eve message for his congregation. As Dr. Edmund Sears worked on his sermon, he was a troubled man. Though it would be another decade before a civil war tore the United States apart, the debate over slavery, compounded by the poverty he saw in his own community, had all but broken the man's spirit. He desperately searched for words to inspire his congregation, but he was having a problem lifting even his own spirit above the depressing scenes that surrounded him.

Sears, then thirty-nine years old, had been educated at Union College in Schenectady, New York, and at Harvard Divinity School. Though the Unitarian church was known for not exposing the divinity of Christ, Sears preached the divine nature of Jesus in his weekly sermons. He believed that Jesus was the Son of God and had died on the cross for man's sins. He also believed that every Christian should be involved in reaching out to the lost, helpless, and poor.

In his community Sears was a force of caring in a world that seemed to concern itself little with the traumas of the hungry or the sick. His burden for the helpless forced him to reach out each day to those Christ called "the least of these." Yet as he worked on writing an uplifting Christmas message, it was the poverty and the hopelessness of the people he touched in the slums that sickened his heart and blocked his progress. He must have wondered how he could write about the Light of the world when the world seemed so very dark.

As Sears struggled, he thumbed through his well-worn Bible. In the second chapter of Luke, the minister was touched by the eighth and ninth verses: "And there were shepherds living out in the fields nearby, keeping watch over their flocks at night. An angel of the Lord appeared to them, and the glory of the Lord shone around them, and they were terrified." After considering the miraculous nature of that long-ago moment, Sears picked up his pen and jotted down a five-verse poem he called "It Came upon the Midnight Clear." He then retrieved from his files another Christmas poem he had written a decade before: "Calm on the list'ning ear of night comes heaven's melodious strains." Beginning his message with his older Christmas poem, he quickly wrote a short sermon and decided to end his Christmas service with the inspired words of his newest poem.

Today Sears's poem turned carol is considered joyful and uplifting. Yet when first delivered, its audience probably saw it as more a charge or challenge than the story of a miraculous birth in a faraway land. While the minister wanted his congregation to celebrate Christmas, he also wanted them to reach out to the poor, to address the nation's social ills, and to consider what they could do as individuals to best reflect the spirit of Christ in their daily lives. In other words, he wanted to see people look to heaven and understand how God needed them to serve man in his name. Nowhere was this message more obvious than in the poem's second verse, one that has been discarded and all but forgotten.

> Yet with the woes of sin and strife
> The world hath suffered long;
> Beneath the angel-strain have rolled
> Two thousand years of wrong;
> And man, at war with man, hears not
> The love song which they bring:
> O hush the noise, ye men of strife,
> And hear the angels sing!

Not only was the beauty and wonder of the Christmas story woven into a lyrical fabric that was rich and meaningful, but Sears also managed to point out that God, in the form of a child, was entering a world that sorely needed his help. He wanted his congregation and the world to hear those cries as he did.

Since Sears was a magazine and newspaper editor in addition to being a preacher, he had the means to bring his new poem to a wider audience than just his church. The *Christian Register,* one of the publications for which Sears penned features, printed "It Came upon the Midnight Clear" in its December 29, 1849, issue. Yet, as is so often the case with inspired work, it would take a second man to breathe lasting life into the poem and make it a Christmas classic.

❄

Richard Storrs Willis was a Yale graduate who had been composing choral pieces since his youth. After graduating from college, the native Bostonian furthered his education in Germany in the 1840s by studying with Moritz Liepizi and Felix Mendelssohn. In 1848 he returned to the United States and became the music critic for the *New York Tribune.*

It came upon the midnight
    clear,
That glorious song of old,
From angels bending near the
    earth
To touch their harps of gold:
"Peace on the earth, good will
    to men,
From heav'n's all gracious King!"
The world in solemn stillness lay
To hear the angels sing.

Still through the cloven skies
    they come
With peaceful wings unfurled,
And still their heav'nly music
    floats
O'er all the weary world:
Above its sad and lowly plains
They bend on hov'ring wing,
And ever o'er its Babel sounds
The blessed angels sing.

And ye, beneath life's crushing
    load
Whose forms are bending low,
Who toil along the climbing way
With painful steps and slow,
Look now! for glad and golden
    hours
Come swiftly on the wing:
O rest beside the weary road
And hear the angels sing.

For lo, the days are hast'ning
    on,
By prophets seen of old,
When with the ever circling
    years
Shall come the time foretold;
When the new heaven and earth
    shall own
The prince of peace their King,
And the whole world send back
    the song
Which now the angels sing.

An avid reader, Willis probably found Sears's poem in the *Christian Register*. Earlier the composer had written a tune he called, simply, "Carol." He discovered that this melody perfectly fit with the lyrics of the poem. Willis's combination of music and words was first published in 1850 with the uninspired title, "Study Number 23." A decade later, using a new, updated arrangement, Willis republished the song as "While Shepherds Watched Their Flocks by Night." It is this second version that is still sung today.

Within a decade of its second printing, "It Came upon the Midnight Clear" had been adopted for use in a wide range of denominational hymnbooks. As the tradition of caroling spread from New England and was adopted throughout the country, the song became a standard for roaming bands of Christmas choirs as well. Yet it wasn't until the twentieth century that the carol would become one of the world's most popular Christmas messages in song.

❈

During World War I, American troops sang "It Came upon the Midnight Clear" throughout France during the holiday season. Thus the song went to war and came home with a generation of men who made it a part of their holiday traditions. Twenty-five years later, U.S. troops took the song back to the front lines of World War II, and entertainers such as Bing Crosby and Dinah Shore performed the haunting carol throughout the Pacific and Europe at U.S.O. shows. For homesick soldiers, no words seemed to voice their own prayers of "peace on earth" as well as those penned by Edmund Sears a century before.

The lasting impact of the song is probably due in part to its last verse. In that stanza Sears begged the world to sing back to heaven the song of hope, peace, love, joy, and salvation. Although "It Came upon the Midnight Clear" has been sung millions of times since Sears first read his poem on a cold Christmas Eve in 1849, most Christians have not yet joined together to cure the world's ills and bring peace to all men. The author's charge, and indeed Jesus' own call, remains largely unanswered.

JINGLE BELLS

"Jingle Bells" is perhaps the most well-known, most sung Christmas carol in America. For millions, this simple little song is as much a part of Christmas as Santa, reindeer, greeting cards, family dinners, evergreen trees, mistletoe, and presents. Yet in one of the season's greatest ironies, "Jingle Bells" does not contain a single reference to the holiday with which it is associated and was actually written for a completely different day of celebration.

※

Medford, Massachusetts native James S. Pierpont had always shown a great deal of musical talent. As a child he not only sang in church, but played the organ. As an adult, Pierpont continued to assist his father, the pastor of Medford's Unitarian church, by working with the choirs and musicians. Around 1840 young Pierpont was given the assignment to write special music for a Thanksgiving service. As James sat in his father's home at 87 Mystic Street contemplating his chore, through a window he watched young men riding their sleds down a hill. Bundling up to ward off the extremely cold weather, Pierpont stepped outside. Caught up in the moment, recalling the many times he had also raced sleds and sleighs sporting bands of merry, jingling bells, he not only watched, but also began to root for the participants. Within an hour he was congratulating the day's winner.

As he stepped back into the house, a melody came to him; while he warmed himself by the fireplace, James hummed the little ditty. Feeling as if this just might be the foundation for the music his father's church program needed, Pierpont threw on his coat and trudged through the snow to the home of Mrs. Otis Waterman. Mrs. Waterman owned the only piano in Medford. When the woman answered the door, James matter-of-factly said, "I have a little tune in my head." The homeowner was familiar with James, knew what he wanted, and immediately stepped aside.

As he sat down at the old instrument and worked out the melody, Mrs. Waterman carefully listened, then said, "That is a merry little jingle you have there." When he finished a few moments later, the woman assured James that the song would catch on around town. Later that evening, Pierpont combined his "jingle" with his observations of the day's sled races and his memories of racing horse-drawn sleighs. Just that quickly a legendary song was born.

James taught his "One Horse Open Sleigh" to the choir at the Medford Church. The fully harmonized arrangement was then presented at the annual Thanksgiving service. Since Thanksgiving was the most important holiday in New England at the time, there was a large audience when "One Horse Open Sleigh" debuted. The number went over so well that many of the church members asked James and the choir to perform it again at the Christmas service. Although a song that mentioned dating and betting on a horse race hardly seemed appropriate for church, "One Horse Open Sleigh" was such a smash at the second performance that scores of Christmas visitors to the Medford sanctuary took it back to their own communities. Due to the fact that they had heard it on the twenty-fifth of December, they taught it to their friends and family as a Christmas song.

Pierpont had no idea his little jingle would have such infectious power; he knew only that folks seemed to like his "winter" song. So when he moved to Savannah, Georgia, he took "One Horse Open Sleigh" with him. He found a publisher for the song in 1857, yet it was not until the *Salem Evening News* did a story about the carol in 1864 that James truly understood he had written something special. By then, the song was fast becoming one of the most popular carols in New England, as well as rushing across the man's adopted South. Within twenty years, "Jingle Bells" was probably the best known caroling song in the country.

❄

As one of the oldest American carols, this "Thanksgiving song," with its rural imagery of snow, sleighs, and jingle bells, has impacted more than a century of Christmas images in greeting cards, books, movies, and scores of Christmas songs.

Pierpont's rather strange Christmas song has been recorded hundreds of times. Benny Goodman, Glenn Miller, and Les Paul all landed on the charts with "Jingle Bells." The most popular recorded version of the song belongs to Bing Crosby and the Andrews Sisters. The

Dashing through the snow
In a one-horse open sleigh
Through the fields we go
Laughing all the way.
Bells on bob-tail ring
Making spirits bright
What fun it is to ride and sing
A sleighing song tonight.

Chorus:
Jingle bells, jingle bells
Jingle all the way,
Oh what fun it is to ride
In a one-horse open sleigh, O
Jingle bells, jingle bells
Jingle all the way,
Oh what fun it is to ride
In a one-horse open sleigh.

A day or two ago
I thought I'd take a ride
And soon Miss Fanny Bright
Was seated by my side;
The horse was lean and lank
Misfortune seemed his lot,

We ran into a drifted bank
And there we got upsot.

Chorus

A day or two ago
The story I must tell
I went out on the snow
And on my back I fell;
A gent was riding by
In a one-horse open sleigh
He laughed at me as
I there sprawling laid
But quickly drove away.

Chorus

Now the ground is white,
Go it while you're young,
Take the girls along
And sing this sleighing song.
Just bet a bob-tailed bay,
Two-forty as his speed,
Hitch him to an open sleigh
And crack! You'll take the lead.

Chorus

little merry jingle can also be found in numerous Hollywood films and television shows, and parts of it have even been used in other Christmas songs. Bobby Helms's hit, "Jingle Bell Rock"—inspired in large part by "Jingle Bells"—has become another well-known modern secular holiday offering.

Today "Jingle Bells" seems to be everywhere. Even though few people have even seen a one-horse open sleigh, millions have jingle bells hanging from their doors at Christmas. Most paintings of Santa show jingling bells adorning his reindeer. And scores of holiday songs and television commercials begin with the jingle of bells. Thanks to James Pierpont and a Thanksgiving request, when people see a picture of snow and a horse-drawn sleigh, their first thought is of Christmas.

JOY TO THE WORLD!

Two brilliant songwriters—although they never met—together created one of Christmas's most lasting songs. Each of these two musical icons ignored the established way of doing things and blazed new trails in every facet of their work. Moreover, the men who brought the song to the world were both trying to bring religious music into a new era. Since they lived a half a world away from each other and were separated by almost a century of time, little did either of these revolutionaries realize that through their collaboration they would create a timeless holiday classic for every age and every audience. As a matter of fact, Isaac Watts and Lowell Mason probably didn't even know they had given the world a Christmas anthem at all.

❋

Isaac Watts was born on July 17, 1674, in Southampton, England. His father, also named Isaac, was a revolutionary protestant church figure in Britain. Strong-willed and stubborn, the elder Watts, a cobbler and tailor by trade, resided in prison when his son was born. He was a criminal nonconformist, having been found guilty of teaching radical ideas that were not approved by the Church of England or established scholars of the time. At a very early age it was obvious that the senior Watts had passed his free-thinking ways onto his son.

Isaac Watts grew up worshiping at Southampton's Above Bar Congregational Church. Most British children who displayed Isaac's intellectual potential would have been assigned to Oxford or Cambridge; yet because he was not a member of the Church of England, Isaac was sent to the Independent Academy at Stoke, Newington. There—no doubt spurred on by his father's example—he continued to display his rebellious nature. Not content to allow things to remain status quo, Watts questioned everything. He demanded to know why he or anyone else should be satisfied with the way things were when they could be so much better. Although he did well in his studies, Isaac left the Academy at the age of twenty after learning Greek, Hebrew, and Latin, and returned home to live with his father.

Like most young people, Watts found church music of the period to be uninspired and monotonous. He saw no joy or emotion in the standards sung by choirs and congregations. Yet while most of the new generation kept quiet, Isaac complained bitterly to his father about the archaic language of the psalms sung in church. The elder Watts, never one to stand on tradition, challenged his son to come up with something better. This challenge initiated a creative burst that would not end until Isaac had composed more than six hundred hymns and hundreds of other poems.

"Behold the Glories of the Lamb" was the first Isaac Watts hymn. It was followed by scores of others. For a while, most of his work was met with contempt; no one wanted new translations of

Joy to the world! the Lord is
  come!
Let earth receive her King;
Let every heart prepare Him room,
And heaven and nature sing,
And heaven and nature sing,
And heaven, and heaven and
  nature sing.

Joy to the earth! the Savior
  reigns!
Let men their songs employ;
While fields and floods, rocks,
  hills and plains
Repeat the sounding joy,
Repeat the sounding joy,
Repeat, repeat the sounding joy.

No more let sins and sorrows
  grow,
Nor thorns infest the ground;
He comes to make His blessings
  flow
Far as the curse is found,
Far as the curse is found,
Far as, far as the curse is found.

He rules the world with truth
  and grace,
And makes the nations prove
The glories of His righteousness,
And wonders of His love,
And wonders of His love,
And wonders, wonders of His
  love.

the Scriptures. Some even viewed young Watts as a heretic or tool of the devil. Yet he refused to give up. He constantly challenged those around him with new songs and new ideas on faith.

After spending several years making his living as a personal tutor, Watts became the assistant to Dr. Isaac Chauncey at Mark Lane Independent Chapel, London. Within three years the now twenty-six-year-old Isaac became the minister. Thanks in part to his work ethic, as well as his new ideas, the church grew rapidly. With his new position and the respect that accompanied it, Isaac was finally able to publish his songs.

Through his hymns and theological writings, Watts became one of the best known clerics in England. Elizabeth Singer—a young woman deeply impressed by the minister's inspired written work—wrote to Isaac and quickly established herself as his biggest fan. She proposed marriage via the mail. When he accepted, Singer anxiously raced to Isaac's side. Rather than cementing a life-long love, this meeting ultimately focused the writer on his work, not on Elizabeth. Singer would later say, "He was only five feet tall, with a shallow face and a hooked nose, prominent cheek bones, small eyes and a deathlike color." Unable to look at the man and see the brilliance that lay just underneath, the woman immediately went back home. Heartbroken, Watts poured himself into his writing, never again seeking the companionship of a woman.

It was while studying Psalm 98 that Isaac was inspired to write his most famous song. In verse four Watts studied the phrase, "Make a joyful noise unto the LORD, all the earth: make a loud noise, and rejoice, and sing praise." Focusing on this verse and the five that followed it, Watts penned a four-stanza poem called "Joy to the World." Set in a common meter, the poem was usually sung to the tune "Come Thou Fount of Every Blessing." Yet because Isaac had dared to rewrite the psalms, few British Christians of the time embraced the song.

Watts did not give up in his efforts to make church music more meaningful to the common man. He continued, in the face of growing criticism, to write and publish new songs. *The Psalms of David Imitated in the Language of the New Testament and Applied to the Christian State and Worship* was released in 1719. This volume, filled with now well-known classics such as "We're Marching to Zion," "When I Survey the Wondrous Cross," "At the Cross," and "This Is the Day the Lord Has Made," would not only be slowly accepted by British Christians but would inspire others like Charles Wesley and John Newton to compose other new Christian songs based on personal experiences. There can be little doubt that Watts's stubborn will and continued efforts to bring Christian music to the common man kept "Joy to the World!" in the public eye long after the writer's death in 1748. It also began a revolution in modern Christian musical thinking.

❉

Forty-four years later, Lowell Mason was born in Orange, New Jersey. As a teen, he directed his church choir and taught at singing schools. Even though many thought of him as musically gifted, Mason didn't see a way to make a living at it. In 1812 the young man moved to Savannah, Georgia, and began a career as a banker. But music hadn't left his soul. In his spare time he also learned harmony, wrote original melodies, and became a student of the composer Handel. With the late German composer as his influence, the banker sent off a book of self-penned music and arrangements to a Boston publisher. When the material was matter-of-factly rejected because the American public wanted new folk music, not classical standards, Mason decided to use his talents only on weekends as a Sunday school teacher and organist at the local Presbyterian church. Imagine his shock when, in 1827, he discovered that not only had his music found a publisher, but that the Handel and Haydn Society of Massachusetts had orders for fifty thousand copies of his songbook! Immediately leaving the South, Lowell Mason moved to Boston.

For the next twenty years Mason was a mover and shaker in New England music circles. Like Isaac Watts, Lowell saw himself as a revolutionary; he was constantly battling the establishment with his own fresh ideas. Schools at the time ignored music, so using his own money, he initiated the first public school music program in Boston. He also became the city's most important music publisher and would eventually write more than six hundred hymns, including "My Faith Looks Up to Thee" and "Nearer My God to Thee."

In 1836, Mason, whose love for the classical composers of Germany had not waned, composed a new melody inspired by two songs from Handel's *Messiah*: "Lift Up Your Head" and "Comfort Ye." Yet when Mason finished his work, he had something brand new, an exuberant ode he called "Antioch" after the Syrian city that was the point of departure for Paul's first two missionary journeys. "Antioch" seemed to beg for words, but it would take the writer a while to find the message to go with his melody. Three years later, in a songbook entitled *Modern Psalmist*, Mason finally linked one of

Watts's psalms-inspired lyrics to his tune. This time the people were ready for "Joy to the World!"

❋

In 1911, Elise Stevenson, who had scored huge chart success during the early days of records with "Shine On, Harvest Moon" and "Are You Sincere?" joined Trinity Choir for a Christmas release of "Joy to the World!" The Victor Records single climbed to number five on the charts and marked the first time that either Watts's or Mason's music had appeared on popular, contemporary music playlists (though "Joy to the World!" would later inspire a rock music hit for a group called "Three Dog Night").

It remains a mystery how this hymn became known as a Christmas carol. Inspired by Old Testament Scripture—with no words alluding to the birth of Jesus other than the phrase, "the Lord is come"—"Joy to the World!" would seem to be a song for all seasons, something to be sung in July as much as December. Nevertheless, for some reason Americans embraced "Joy to the World!" as a holiday standard. Perhaps, because of its jubilant spirit, it just "felt" like a Christmas song!

"Joy to the World!" is one of today's most loved Christmas carols. Yet because it does not use as its inspiration anything from the first four gospels of the New Testament, it also stands as a unique non-Christmas Christmas standard. Perhaps that is fitting, since both Isaac Watts and Lowell Mason strove to push the envelope in order to get people to see Scripture and music in a whole new way. Watts and Mason knew, and we should remember, that Christians should exude joy each and every day because the "Lord is come."

MARY, DID YOU KNOW?

*N*o Christmas song written in the past three decades has provoked the kind of response that "Mary, Did You Know?" has. Buddy Green's simple and touching melody certainly deserves some of the credit for the song's popularity and acceptance, but most people who hear the song are really drawn to the unique perspective found in Mark Lowry's dynamic lyrics. Yet this song's gift to the world might have been lost forever if a set of loving parents had not chosen to believe in the promise and potential God placed in their child.

❄

Mark Lowry is one of the most interesting personalities in gospel music. A singer with the Gaither Vocal Band, a humorist, and a songwriter, Mark never stops moving. He seems to have the energy of three fifth graders and the curiosity of a dozen four-year-old children. Probably because the Lord knows the world couldn't handle more than one Mark Lowry at a time, there is no one like him. One observer called Lowry a "raccoon in human form" and everyone wonders how his parents ever kept up with him. Yet it is his parents, once run ragged by Mark's energy, that deserve a big part of the credit for this man's greatest song.

Mark started singing almost before he learned to talk. As a preschooler he was already belting out solos in the grade school choir. By third grade he was singing the lead part in the Easter musical. Yet even though he constantly seemed to be in the school spotlight and living in the perfect American family environment at home, there were rough waters and some tough times just ahead.

Mark stood out in teachers' eyes for more than his singing; he was often a problem in the classroom. During his first years of elementary school, Lowry was diagnosed as hyperactive and placed on medication. At about that same time it became apparent that the boy had absolutely no athletic ability. To many adults and kids, Mark appeared to be little more than an energetic klutz—an out of control mini-tornado. Rather than allow their son to be sidetracked and dismissed as a hopeless cause, Mark's parents made sure that this "curse" was looked at as a blessing. They emphasized the positive.

The Lowrys assured Mark that God had a plan for his life and that his uniqueness was a part of it. Instead of trying to make him act just like all the other kids, the Lowrys allowed Mark to exploit his curiosity and his energy. He loved performing, so they put him on every stage that would take him—everything from church programs to community musicals. It was at the National Quartet Convention where Lowry not only received his biggest break but also his calling.

At the convention Lowry sang in front of fifteen thousand gospel music fans. The audience couldn't get enough of him.

They loved everything about the funny, talented kid. Seeing the potential that once only his folks had seen, Benson Records signed Mark. Over the next few years he cut inspirational albums with the likes of the London Symphony Orchestra and was so busy with his musical career that he had to finish junior high and high school via correspondence courses.

In 1984, Mark was living in Houston. Feeling blessed to have Lowry in his flock, Mark's pastor asked him to write the program for the living Christmas tree choir presentation. The group traditionally sang familiar holiday carols, so Lowry's job was to write the bridges that connected one song to another. It was while he was working on the project that Mark considered what it would have been like to have been Jesus' mother.

"When I wrote this thing about Mary," Mark explained, "I began by thinking I was interviewing her on her thoughts of being a mother to Jesus. A couple of the lines I wrote really stood out, like 'when you kiss your little baby, you've kissed the face of God.' I just thought this needed to be a song."

Keeping the perspective of a reporter doing a story on Jesus from Mary's viewpoint, Mark penned a poem that sent chills up his spine. Still, taking those powerful lyrics and turning them into a full-blown song was a bigger challenge than even he could have expected. Although he gave the words to a solid music writer, he wasn't happy with the results; the melody didn't have the right feel. Filing "Mary, Did You Know?" away, Mark decided to wait on the Lord's timing rather than put his lyrics to music that failed to move him.

❋

In 1988, after Gary McSpadden left the Gaither Vocal Band, Bill Gaither was looking for a replacement to fill the void in his quartet. After watching a video of Mark Lowry onstage, not

Mary, did you know, that your
   baby boy
Would one day walk on water?
Mary, did you know, that your
   baby boy
Would save our sons and
   daughters?

Did you know, that your baby
   boy
Has come to make you new?
This Child that you delivered,
   will soon deliver you.

Mary, did you know, that your
   baby boy
Will give sight to the blind man?
Mary, did you know, that your
   baby boy
Would calm a storm with His
   hand?

Did you know, that your baby boy
Has walked where angels trod
And when you kiss your little
baby, you've kissed the face
   of God?
Oh, Mary, did you know?
Mary, did you know?

The blind will see, the deaf will
   hear,
The dead will live again
The lame will leap, the dumb
   will speak
Praises of the Lamb?

Mary, did you know, that your
   baby boy
Is Lord of all creation?
Mary, did you know, that your
   baby boy
Will one day rule the nations?

Did you know, that your baby
   boy
Was Heaven's perfect Lamb
And this sleeping Child you're
   holding
Is the Great I Am
Oh, Mary.

only was Gaither impressed with Mark's singing, he thought the young man could bring a great deal of Christian humor to the group's performances. When Bill called, Mark packed his bags.

Mark had been with the band for two years when Buddy Green joined them. A talented musician, Buddy was also a songwriter who was beginning to hit stride and produce some very strong work. Mark decided to share "Mary, Did You Know?" with Buddy.

Rather than pull Green to one side and share the story behind the song, Mark wrote a short note over the top of the lyrics: *Buddy, here are some God-inspired words. Please add some beautiful music and make it a profitable hit.* The memo was meant as a joke, but Green took both the note and his job seriously. He set the lyrics aside for a couple of weeks, then went to work. When he finished, he called Mark on the phone and sang the song to him. Lowry loved it and within a week they had put together a "jam box" demo to give to one of their favorite artists.

Their pick for the song was impressed as well. When "Mary, Did You Know?" was originally cut by Christian sensation Michael English, the writing duo felt blessed, but they really didn't expect anyone else to jump on the bandwagon. Then country singer Kathy Mattea heard the Lowry-Green number and recorded it next. Scores of other acts quickly took the song into the studio, including Natalie Cole. Thanks to this exposure, "Mary, Did You Know?" was soon adopted by choirs and soloists. Even President Bill Clinton declared it was his favorite Christmas song. For the first time in decades, a new Christmas song had become an important facet of traditional holiday celebrations. For the first time ever, southern gospel music had given the world a Christmas carol.

There can be no doubt that Mark Lowry was born different. The things that make him unique—his energy and his curiosity—could have held him back like so many others. He could have been forced to conform, to be like everyone else. Yet because his problems were viewed as gifts by his parents, Mark thrived. Looking at the world through his unique, God-given perspective led him to think of one of the world's most familiar stories in a new light. "Mary, Did You Know?" a song like no other Christmas carol ever penned, written about a mother like no other, came from the hand of a man like no other.

O COME, ALL YE FAITHFUL

O Come, All Ye Faithful" has been sung in churches of all denominations for almost two hundred years and sung in Catholic masses for much longer. In the past century it has been recorded hundreds of times by some of the greatest entertainers in history. It is even one of the few traditional religious carols to land on the record charts, making it to the top ten three times. It has been translated into more than 150 languages, used in thousands of cantatas and musical productions, and called by some critics "the greatest carol ever written." It is amazing, therefore, that the song's author remained unknown until just after World War II.

For several hundred years it was believed that the person who wrote "O Come, All Ye Faithful" was an unknown cleric from the Middle Ages or even before. Legend had it that Saint Bonaventura had penned the words. So it came as quite a shock when English scholar Maurice Frost discovered seven "O Come, All Ye Faithful" transcripts written by hand and signed by an English Catholic priest named John Francis Wade. How

Wade's authorship of this great carol remained unknown for more than two hundred years is a mystery that may never be solved, yet the story behind how the Catholic cleric came to write "O Come, All Ye Faithful" is one of adventure.

❉

John Wade was a man of God caught in the middle of a Holy War. In 1745, at the age of thirty-five, Wade's life was on the line. Strife between the Church of England and the Roman Catholic church was at an all-time high. Many practicing Catholics were forced to take their faith underground. To avoid prison or death, many priests fled Britain, including John Wade. He made his way to Douay, France, where, in a city inundated by English Catholics and those who opposed the British royal family, Wade was given an important job. Since many Catholic Church records were lost during the conflict in England, Wade was to research and identify historical church music, then carefully record and preserve it for future generations. The man took his job very seriously, leaving no stone unturned in his efforts to save anything of historical or spiritual value. Little could he have realized just how profound and long-reaching his work would be.

A calligrapher by training, as well as a skilled musician, Wade saved not only historical church songs, he then organized and distributed them to Catholic churches throughout Europe. Through his beautifully detailed drawings and manuscripts, the priest reintroduced many forgotten songs to masses across France and beyond.

Wade reclaimed old pieces but also was inspired to write new hymns. As a Catholic cleric, it was only natural that he compose his new works in Latin. In or around 1750, Wade put the finishing touches on what would become his most famous tune, "Adeste Fideles." He published it in his own book, *Cantus Diversi*, the next year. A decade later he completed and put lyrics to his melody. Yet somehow, even though it was published at least two different times with John Wade credited as being the composer, credit for writing "Adeste Fideles" remained a mystery when Frederrick Oakeley translated the original lyrics into English in 1841. At about that time, many legends about the song's author began to take seed, but none of them named John Wade.

In the 1800s, Saint Bonaventura somehow emerged as the original writer of the song. There may be at least some fact in this legend. It is possible that Wade came across the writings of Bonaventura when he was doing his work in France, and that Bonaventura's songs might have inspired or influenced Wade's work during this period.

The next—and often still repeated—legend began in London around 1860, when "O Come, All Ye Faithful" was performed in the Portuguese embassy. The organist, Vincent Novello, informed his audience that a man named John Redding had composed the melody. While Redding seemed to have taken credit for writing "O Come, All Ye Faithful," Wade's manuscripts, penned more than a century before Redding's birth, completely void his claim. The song was, however, published by Redding and is often called the "Portuguese Hymn." Because of this, many believed that the Englishman wrote the music, but that an unknown man from Portugal penned the words. The Bonaventura and Redding tales are just two of many that supposedly pin down the origins of "O Come, All Ye Faithful."

In America, as in most of the world, the song was adopted by many Christian churches before 1900. It was also one of the focal points of the caroling movement that swept the country. Mobile

O come, all ye faithful, joyful
    and triumphant,
Come ye, O come ye, to
    Bethlehem;
Come and behold Him, born
    the King of angels:

Chorus:
O come, let us adore Him,
O come, let us adore Him,
O come, let us adore Him,
Christ, the Lord.

True God of true God, Light
    from Light Eternal,
Lo, he shuns not the Virgin's
    womb;
Son of the Father, begotten, not
    created;

Chorus

Sing, choirs of angels, sing in
    exultation,
Sing, all ye citizens of heaven
    above!
Glory to God, all glory in the
    highest:

Chorus

See how the shepherds,
    summoned to His cradle,
Leaving their flocks, draw nigh
    to gaze;
We too will thither bend our
    joyful footsteps:

Chorus

Child, for us sinners poor and
    in the manger,
We would embrace Thee, with
    love and awe;
Who would not love Thee, lov-
    ing us so dearly?

Chorus

Yea, Lord, we greet Thee, born
    this happy morning,
Jesus, to Thee be glory given;
Word of the Father, now in
    flesh appearing:

Chorus

choirs, going from house to house singing songs of the Christmas season, always sang "O Come, All Ye Faithful." More often than not, each performance closed with the mighty chorus.

During the 1905 Christmas season, the greatest American vocal group of the period, the Peerless Quartet, recorded and released the carol. At a time when radio had yet to introduce music to the masses, thousands of copies of this Christmas single were sold. The single even hit number seven on the "National Hit Parade." The only Christmas recording among the more than one hundred Peerless Quartet hit songs, "O Come, All Ye Faithful" became the group's signature holiday anthem.

The world's most famous Irish tenor, John McCormack, took John Wade's carol to number two on the national playlists in 1915. A decade later the American Glee Club proved again that "O Come, All Ye Faithful" was still America's favorite Christmas song. In a medium where very few Christian songs found universal favor, the song remained the most beloved holiday offering until Bing Crosby cut "White Christmas." Of course, on that same album release, Crosby also placed his own version of "O Come, All Ye Faithful." It was at that time that Maurice Frost finally sifted through all the legends and uncovered the song's real writer, finally granting John Francis Wade the credit he so richly deserved.

Wade's authorship and genius *should* be acknowledged. Even though he was living in a time of great conflict between various branches of the Christian Church, forced to give up the country he loved as a sacrifice of faith, and made to work long hours trying to preserve church records that others were attempting to erase for all time, Wade fully revelled in his role as a servant of his Lord. In every word and verse of "O Come, All Ye Faithful," the composer's faith is not just verified, it is magnified. At a time when the church was literally at war, only someone who truly believed in the holiness of Christ could have written a carol that would bring all Christians together to the same place each Christmas—bowing before Christ the Lord!

O Come, O Come, Emmanuel

"O Come, O Come, Emmanuel" is probably the oldest Christmas carol still sung today. This popular hymn dates back to the ninth century and represents an important and ancient series of services celebrated by the Catholic church. It also presents the different biblical roles that the church believed Jesus fulfilled. The universal nature of faith presented in this song can now be best seen by the fact that it has crossed over from a hymn sung in Latin and used in only formal Catholic masses to a carol translated into scores of languages and embraced by every Christian denomination in the world.

The writer of "O Come, O Come, Emmanuel" is unknown. He was no doubt a monk or priest who penned the words before 800 A.D. He was also a scholar with a rich knowledge of both the Old and New Testaments. Once completed, the hymn was evidently picked up by many European churches and monasteries and became an intensely important part of the church. Yet for fifty-one weeks of each year it was ignored, saved for a single week of Advent vespers leading up to the celebration of Christ's birth.

In its original form, "O Come, O Come, Emmanuel" was known as a song of the "Great Antiphons" or "Great O's." The initial Latin text, framed in the original seven different verses, represented the different biblical views of the Messiah. One verse per day was sung or chanted during the last seven days before Christmas.

Much more than the very simple, almost monotone melody employed at the time, the words painted a rich illustration of the many biblical prophesies fulfilled by Christ's birth. So the story of "O Come, O Come, Emmanuel" is really a condensed study of the Bible's view of the Messiah—who he was, what he represented and why he had to come to Earth. Even to this day, if one is a proficient Bible student, the song's lyrics reveal the unfolding story of the Messiah.

For the people of the Dark Ages—few of whom read or had access to the Bible—the song was one of the few examples of the full story of how the New and Old Testament views of the Messiah came together in the birth and life of Jesus. Because it brought the story of Christ the Savior to life during hundreds of years of ignorance and darkness, "O Come, O Come, Emmanuel" ranks as one of the most important songs in the history of the Christian faith.

The song owes its worldwide acceptance to a man named John Mason Neale. Born on January 24, 1818, this Anglican priest was educated at Trinity College in Cambridge. Brilliant, a man who could write and speak more than twenty languages, he should have been destined for greatness. Yet many feared his intelligence and insight. At the time, church leaders thought he was too evangelical, too progressive, and too much a free-thinker to be allowed to influence the masses. So rather than get a pastorate in London, Neale was sent by the church to the Madiera Islands off the northwest coast of Africa. Pushed out of the spotlight and given the position of warden in an all but forgotten locale, it was expected that he and his ideas would never again find root in England. Yet Neale·refused to give up on God or his own calling. On a salary of just twenty-seven pounds a year he established the Sisterhood of St. Margaret. From this order he began an orphanage, a school for girls, and a house of refuge for prostitutes. And these noble ministries were just the beginning.

When he wasn't ministering to those who could truly be called "the least of these," the often frail and sickly Neale reviewed every facet of Scripture and Scripture-based writing he could find. It was during these studies that he came across the Latin chant, "O Come, O Come, Emmanuel" in a book called *Psalteroium Cantionum Catholicarum.* Seizing on the importance of the song's inspired text, Neale translated the words into English. Interestingly, in his initial work, the lyrics began, "Draw nigh, draw nigh, Emmanuel."

The tune that went with Neale's translation had been used for some years in Latin text versions of the song. "Veni Emmanuel" was a fifteenth century processional that originated in a community of French Franciscan nuns living in Lisbon, Portugal. Neale's translation of the lyrics coupled with "Veni Emmanuel" was first published in the 1850s in England. Within twenty-five years, Neale's work, later cut to five verses and called "O Come, O Come, Emmanuel," grew in popularity throughout Europe and America.

Although sung countless times each Christmas, much of the song's rich meaning seems to have been set aside or lost. While both men—the ancient monk and the exiled priest—would probably be amazed that any still remember their work, the

O come, o come, Emmanuel,
And ransom captive Israel,
That mourns in lonely exile here
Until the Son of God appear.

Chorus:
Rejoice! Rejoice! Emmanuel
Shall come to thee, O Israel.

O come, thou rod of Jesse, free
Thine own from Satan's
    tyranny;
From depths of hell thy people
    save
And give them vict'ry o'er the
    grave

Chorus

O come, O Dayspring, come
    and cheer
Our spirits by thine advent here;

And drive away the shades of
    night
And pierce the clouds and bring
    us light.

Chorus

O come, Thou Key of David,
    come
And open wide our heavenly
    home
Make safe the way that leads
    on high
And close the path to misery.

Chorus

O come, O come, Adonai,
Who in thy glorious majesty
From Sinai's mountain, clothes
    in awe,
Gavest thy folk the elder law.

Chorus

fact that few realize the full impact of the words would no doubt disappoint them greatly. After all, to sing a song and not feel the power and majesty of its meaning trivializes both the music and the lyrics.

The first verse of the song is taken from Isaiah 7:14 and Matthew 1:23. It introduces Emmanuel—"God with us"—and Israel as a symbol for the Christian world, held captive on a dark and sinful Earth.

Isaiah 11 serves as the theme for the verse that begins "O come, thou rod of Jesse, free" (in some translations this is called the "Branch of Jesse"). In it the rod of Jesse represents Christ, who is the only one who can defeat Satan and bring eternal life to all those who follow him.

"O come, O Dayspring, come and cheer" presents the image of the morning star, a concept that can be traced back to Malachi 4:2. In this verse, the song states that the coming Savior will bring justice, honesty, and truth. He will enlighten and cast out darkness. As Malachi promises: "The sun of righteousness will rise with healing in its wings."

The lyrics then turn to "O come, thou key of David," a reference to Isaiah 22:22. The words in this verse explain that the newborn King holds the key to the heavenly kingdom and there is no way to get into the kingdom but through him.

The verse that begins "O come, O come, Adonai"

(in some texts this reads "O come, thou wisdom from on high") centers on the source of true wisdom. This comes only from God through his Son. Through the Savior, this wisdom can reach around the world and bring peace and understanding to all men. Thus, Christ's teachings and examples fulfilled all Old Testament prophesies.

Even today, when sung in a public hall by a small group of carolers or during a television special, the original chants of long forgotten monks can almost be heard. Although translated into scores of languages and sung in a wild variety of styles and arrangements, the simplistic yet spiritual nature of the song remains intact. It is reverent, a tribute to not only the birth of God's child but also to the fulfillment of God's promise to deliver his children from the world. In this simple but brilliant song, the echoed voices of clerics from the past gently urge today's world to accept and worship the King who fulfills God's greatest promise to his children.

O HOLY NIGHT

The strange and fascinating story of "O Holy Night" began in France, yet eventually made its way around the world. This seemingly simple song, inspired by a request from a clergyman, would not only become one of the most beloved anthems of all time, it would mark a technological revolution that would forever change the way people were introduced to music.

In 1847, Placide Cappeau de Roquemaure was the commissionaire of wines in a small French town. Known more for his poetry than his church attendance, it probably shocked Placide when his parish priest asked the commissionaire to pen a poem for Christmas mass. Nevertheless, the poet was honored to share his talents with the church.

In a dusty coach traveling down a bumpy road to France's capitol city, Cappeau considered the priest's request. The poem obviously had to be religious, focus on Christmas, and be based on Scripture. Using the gospel of Luke as his guide, Cappeau imagined witnessing the birth of Jesus in Bethlehem.

Thoughts of being present on the blessed night inspired him. By the time the commissionaire arrived in Paris, the poem "Cantique de Noel" had been completed.

Moved by his own work, Cappeau determined that his "Cantique de Noel" was not just a poem, but a song in need of a master musician's hand. Not musically inclined himself, the poet turned to one of his friends, Adolphe Charles Adams, for help.

Adolphe, born in 1803, was five years older than Cappeau. The son of a well-known classical musician, Adolphe had studied at the Paris Conservatoire. By 1829 he had produced his first one-act opera, *Pierre et Catherine*. He followed this success with *Richard en Palestine*. Adams then scored acclaim with ballets such as *Faust, La Fille du Danube,* and *La Jolie Fille de Gand*. His talent and fame brought requests to write works for orchestras and ballets all around the world. Yet the lyrics that his friend Cappeau gave him must have challenged the composer in a fashion unlike anything he had received from London, Berlin, or St. Petersburg.

As Adolphe studied "Cantique de Noel," he couldn't help but note its overtly spiritual lyrics embracing the birth of a Savior. A man of Jewish ancestry, these words represented a holiday he didn't celebrate and a man he did not view as the Son of God. Nevertheless, moved by more than friendship, Adams quickly and diligently went to work, attempting to marry an original score to Cappeau's beautiful words. Adams's finished work pleased both poet and priest. It was performed just three weeks later at a midnight mass on Christmas Eve. Neither the wine commissionaire nor the composer was prepared for what happened next.

Initially, "Cantique de Noel" was wholeheartedly accepted by the church in France and the song quickly found its way into various Catholic Christmas services. But when Placide Cappeau walked away from the church and became a part of the socialist movement, and church leaders discovered that Adolphe Adams was a Jew, the song—which had quickly grown to be one of the most beloved Christmas songs in France—was suddenly and uniformly denounced by the church. The heads of the French Catholic church of the time deemed "Cantique de Noel" as unfit for church services because of its lack of musical taste and "total absence of the spirit of religion." Yet even as the church tried to bury the Christmas song, the French people continued to sing it, and a decade later a reclusive American writer brought it to a whole new audience halfway around the world.

Born May 13, 1813, in Boston, John Sullivan Dwight was a graduate of Harvard College and Divinity school. He became a Unitarian minister in Northampton, Massachusetts, but for inexplicable reasons grew physically ill each time he had to address his congregation. These panic attacks magnified to such an extent that Dwight often locked himself in his home, scared to venture out in public. It soon became obvious he would be unable to continue in the ministry.

Gifted and bright, Dwight sought other ways to use his talent. An accomplished writer, he used his skills to found *Dwight's Journal of Music*. For three decades he quietly edited the publication. Although he couldn't face crowds of people, some of the most gifted musicians and music lovers in the Northeast were inspired by his confident writing. As he looked for new material to review, Dwight read "Cantique de Noel" in French. The former minister quickly fell in love with the carol's haunting lyrics.

Not only did Dwight feel that this wonderful Christmas song needed to be introduced to America, he saw something else in

O holy night, the stars are
    brightly shining;
It is the night of the dear Savior's
    birth!
Long lay the world in sin and
    error pining,
Till He appeared and the soul
    felt its worth.
A thrill of hope, the weary soul
    rejoices,
For yonder breaks a new and
    glorious morn.

Chorus:
Fall on your knees, O hear the
    angel voices!
O night divine, O night when
    Christ was born!
O night, O holy night, O night
    divine!

Led by the light of faith serenely
    beaming,
With glowing hearts by His
    cradle we stand.

So led by light of a star sweetly
    gleaming,
Here came the wise men from
    Orient land.
The King of kings lay thus in
    lowly manger,
In all our trials born to be our
    friend!

Chorus

Truly He taught us to love one
    another;
His law is love and His Gospel
    is peace.
Chains shall He break for the
    slave is our brother
And in His Name all oppression
    shall cease.
Sweet hymns of joy in grateful
    chorus raise we,
Let all within us praise His holy
    Name!

Chorus

the song that moved him beyond the story of the birth of Christ. An ardent abolitionist, Dwight strongly identified with the lines, "Truly he taught us to love one another; his law is love and his gospel is peace. Chains shall he break, for the slave is our brother; and in his name all oppression shall cease!" The text supported Dwight's own view of slavery in the South. The writer believed that Christ came to free all men, and in this song all men would be confronted with the fact.

Keeping the original meaning intact, Dwight translated the lyrics into a hauntingly beautiful English text. Published in his magazine and in several songbooks of the period, "O Holy Night" quickly found favor in America, especially in the North during the Civil War.

※

Back in France, even though the song had been banned from the church for almost two decades, many commoners still sang "Cantique de Noel" at home. Legend has it that on Christmas Eve 1871, in the midst of fierce fighting between the armies of Germany and France during the Franco-Prussian War, a French soldier suddenly jumped out of his muddy trench. Both sides stared at the seemingly crazed man. Boldly standing with no weapon in his hands or at his side, he lifted his eyes to the heavens and sang, "Minuit, chrétiens, C'est l'heure solennelle Où l'Homme Dieu descendit jusqu'à nous," the beginning of "Cantique de Noel."

After completing all three verses, a German infantryman climbed out of his hiding place and answered with, "Vom Himmel hoch, da komm' ich her. Ich bring' euch gute neue Mär, Der guten Mär bring' ich so viel, Davon ich sing'n und sagen will," the beginning of Martin Luther's robust "From Heaven above to Earth I Come."

The story goes that the fighting stopped for the next twenty-four hours while the men on both sides observed a temporary peace in honor of Christmas day. Perhaps this story had a part in the French church once again embracing "Cantique de Noel" as being worthy of inclusion in holiday services.

❄

Adams had been dead for many years and Cappeau and Dwight were old men when on Christmas Eve 1906, Reginald Fessenden—a thirty-three-year-old university professor in Pittsburgh and former chief chemist for Thomas Edison—did something long thought impossible. Using a new type of generator, Fessenden spoke into a microphone and, for the first time in history, a man's voice was broadcast over the airwaves: "And it came to pass in those days, that there went out a decree from Caesar Augustus, that all the world should be taxed," he began in a clear, strong voice, hoping he was reaching across the distances he supposed he would.

Shocked radio operators on ships and astonished wireless owners at newspapers sat slack-jawed as their normal, coded impulses, heard over tiny speakers, were interrupted by a professor reading from the gospel of Luke. To the few who caught this broadcast, it must have seemed like a miracle—hearing a voice somehow turned into electrical waves and transmitted to those far away. Some might have believed they were hearing the voice of an angel.

Fessenden was probably unaware of the sensation he was causing on ships and in offices; he couldn't know that men and women were rushing to their wireless units to catch this Christmas Eve miracle. Yet after finishing his recitation of the birth of Christ, Fessenden picked up his violin and played "O Holy Night," the first song ever sent through the air via radio waves. When the carol ended, so did the broadcast—but not before music had found a new medium that would take it around the world.

❄

Since that first rendition at a small Christmas mass in 1847, "O Holy Night" has been sung millions of times in churches in every corner of the world. And since the moment a handful of people first heard it played over the radio, the carol has gone on to become one of the entertainment industry's most recorded and played spiritual songs. Total sales for the thousands of different versions of the carol are in the tens of millions. This incredible work—requested by a forgotten parish priest, written by a poet who would later split from the church, given soaring music by a Jewish composer, and brought to Americans to serve as much as a tool to spotlight the sinful nature of slavery as tell the story of the birth of a Savior—has grown to become one of the most beautiful, inspired pieces of music ever created.

O LITTLE TOWN OF BETHLEHEM

*O*n December 24, 1865, Phillips Brooks was a half a world away from home and feeling like an older man than his thirty years. Already recognized as one of the most dynamic Christian voices in America, it was Brooks, only six years into his ministry, who had been called upon in May to give the funeral message over President Abraham Lincoln. That solemn honor, in tandem with leading the congregation of Philadelphia's Holy Trinity Church through the bloody years of the Civil War, had taken its toll. Worn out and badly needing a spiritual rebirth, Brooks took a sabbatical and left the United States to tour the Middle East.

On Christmas Eve in Jerusalem, the American felt an urge to get away from the hundreds of other pilgrims who had journeyed to the Holy Land for the holidays. Although warned that he might encounter thieves, the preacher borrowed a horse and set out across the desolate and unforgiving countryside. For many peaceful hours he was alone with his thoughts as he studied a land that had changed little since

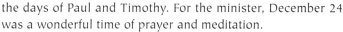

the days of Paul and Timothy. For the minister, December 24 was a wonderful time of prayer and meditation.

At dusk, a sudden sense of awe fell over Brooks. Under a clear sky, the first stars just beginning to emerge, he rode into the still tiny and remote village of Bethlehem. He recalled the story of the birth of his Savior, and by being present in the place in which Jesus was born, was able to add vivid detail to the familiar tale in Scripture. The great speaker was all but speechless as he considered the heavenly King, born in such modest surroundings. There, on streets almost unchanged since biblical times, Brooks felt as if he were surrounded by the spirit of the first Christmas. He would later tell his family and friends that the experience was so overpowering that it would forever be "singing in my soul."

Like the path from Jerusalem to Bethlehem, Phillips Brooks's own life had often been rocky and winding. At the age of twenty-two, the Harvard graduate was a struggling teacher at Boston's Latin School. Though his knowledge of his subject was great, he found it all but impossible to teach because his students wouldn't devote the effort Brooks felt was needed to master the course. Frustrated, Brooks gave up.

Lacking faith in himself, the young man turned to prayer and Bible study in an effort to find his place in the world. Still unsure of his future, Brooks entered the Episcopal Theological Seminary and began pastoral studies. After graduating in 1859, he began his ministry in Philadelphia.

What Phillips Brooks had lacked in the classroom, he made up for in the pulpit. His messages were powerful and dramatic. In 1861 he was called to lead the congregation of the Holy Trinity Church in Philadelphia. No sooner had he unpacked his Bible than Brooks contacted well-known real estate agent Lewis Redner. The preacher convinced supersalesman Redner to serve

O little town of Bethlehem,
   how still we see thee lie
Above thy deep and dreamless
   sleep the silent stars go by
Yet in thy dark streets shineth,
   the everlasting light
The hopes and fears of all the
   years are met in thee tonight.

For Christ is born of Mary, and
   gathered all above
While mortals sleep the angels
   keep their watch of wondering
   love
O morning stars together,
   proclaim the holy birth.
And praises sing to God the king,
   and peace to men on earth.

How silently, how silently, the
   wondrous gift is given
So God imparts to human hearts
   the blessings of his heaven
No ear may hear his coming,
   but in this world of sin
Where meek souls will receive
   him still, the dear Christ
   enters in.

O holy Child of Bethlehem,
   descend to us we pray
Cast out our sin and enter in,
   be born in us today
We hear the Christmas angels,
   the great glad tidings tell
O come to us, abide with us,
   our lord Emmanuel.

as Sunday school superintendent and organist at Trinity. Together Brooks and Redner welcomed thirty children to their first Sunday morning class. Within a year—thanks to Brooks's preaching and Redner's music—the Sunday and Wednesday services were filled to overflowing and one thousand children were attending Sunday school each week. Over the next two years those numbers continued to build.

Yet even as Holy Trinity grew and his fame spread far and wide, Brooks was growing physically and spiritually tired. By 1863, in the midst of the Civil War, the national spirit was dying almost as quickly as the soldiers on the battlefields. Everyone knew someone who had been killed or gravely injured in the conflict. Scores of women in the church wore black as they mourned the loss of a husband or son. While the preacher tried to fight it, darkness fell over every facet of the services. Brooks was severely taxed each time he stood in front of his congregation. They wanted him to be inspirational, to believe that the good things in life they had once known would someday be theirs again. They wanted an end to the war. Yet even though he made a valiant effort, the preacher couldn't give his flock what they needed most: peace.

When the war finally ended, the visibly fatigued Brooks felt that the sweetness of life and the soul would soon return to his flock. Yet the pain only intensified when President Lincoln was assassinated. Although he was not Lincoln's pastor, and felt ill-prepared to preside over the ceremony, Brooks was asked to speak at Lincoln's funeral because of his reputation as an orator. Digging deep, he found words to fit the moment, but seeing a great leader senselessly slain and the exhaustion of the effort itself left him void of everything he needed as a pastor. In an attempt to rediscover and restore his own faith, he left the pulpit to visit the Holy Land. It was a trip that dramatically changed his life and renewed his calling. The dark days ended, the joy of living returned, and his positive attitude again became apparent in his every step and word.

Returning from his sabbatical with renewed vigor, Brooks tried to relate to his congregation the incredible experience of walking where Jesus had walked. Yet Brooks's unparalleled oratory still fell short. For the next three years, "the singing in [his] soul" remained strong, but his inability to share the stirring imagery haunted him to such an extent that he wrote the following note in his journal:

> Before dark we rode out of town to the field where they say the shepherds saw the star. It is a fenced piece of ground with a cave in it, in which, strangely enough, they put the shepherds. . . . somewhere in those fields we rode through, the shepherds must have been. As we passed, the shepherds were still keeping watch over their flocks.

He also added this experience to the log of his trip:

> I was standing in the old church in Bethlehem, close to the spot where Jesus was born, when the whole church was ringing hour after hour with the splendid hymns of praise to God, how again and again it seemed as if I could hear voices I know well, telling each other of the Saviour's birth.

Still, even after reliving this rich experience, inspiration about how to convey those amazing moments to his flock did not visit the preacher.

When Brooks looked ahead to the holiday season of 1868, he again thought of riding into Bethlehem at dusk and the church service that had followed. This time, he didn't force the words out, he simply relived the experience and jotted down the lines that seemed to float into his head. His thoughts soon took the form of a poem. When he finished, he hurried to share it with Lewis Redner.

While reading the simple words, Redner finally understood the power of what Brooks had experienced in the Holy Land. To further share this message, the organist tried to compose music to accompany the poem. For hours he struggled at the piano. Finally, on December 24, as Redner went to bed, he was forced to admit he had failed.

Just as Brooks had been unable to find dynamic oratory to fully describe what he had experienced in Bethlehem, Redner was unable to compose a majestic rhapsody to carry the preacher's simple words. It was only in his bed, long after he had given up his efforts, that the organist found an unadorned and straightforward tune. Rubbing the sleep from his eyes, Redner discovered the tune given to him in slumber perfectly fit Phillips Brooks's words. As if blessed by God himself, on Christmas morning "O Little Town of Bethlehem" was complete.

For the next six years "O Little Town of Bethlehem" was a Philadelphia favorite. Printed in cheap leaflet form, almost every church in the city used it during their Christmas services. In 1874, William Huntington published Brooks's impressions and Redner's music in *The Church Porch* music collection. By the time of Phillips Brooks's death in 1893, "O Little Town of Bethlehem" had become one of the most beloved Christmas carols in the world.

Phillips Brooks is now recognized as the greatest American preacher of the nineteenth century. His first volume of sermons sold more than two hundred thousand copies when released in 1878 and is still read and studied today. There is even a building named for the preacher at Harvard University.

Yet it is the songwriter, not the preacher, whose work millions now know and cherish. It is the simple language of a common traveler in search of spiritual renewal that continues to touch lives today. In a sermon Brooks once said, "It is while you are patiently toiling at the little tasks of life that the meaning and shape of the great whole of life dawns on you." On a horse, in a tiny village, a half a world away from his home and family, the meaning of Phillips Brooks's life and the purpose behind his work were brought into sharp focus. Since that time, millions have been blessed because of his ability to share his revelation with the world.

RUDOLPH THE RED-NOSED REINDEER

*I*n 1938, as the Great Depression wound down and even as the prospect of better times loomed on the horizon, Bob May was looking toward another bleak Christmas. An advertising copywriter for Montgomery Wards, living on a meager salary, May was on the brink of bankruptcy and exhaustion. After fighting cancer for two long years, his wife, Evelyn, was losing the battle. Staring into each other's eyes, they both knew she wouldn't last long. Their daughter knew something was wrong too.

On a cold December night, after visiting her bedridden, emaciated mother, their four-year-old, Barbara, climbed up into her father's lap. "Why isn't my mommy just like everybody else's mommy?" she solemnly asked.

How could he explain to a small child that her critically ill mother wanted to play with Barbara, read her stories and— more than anything in the world—be with her for every important moment in life? How could he tell an innocent girl that illness and death were a part of life? That Evelyn wanted to be like other mothers, but illness had excluded her from all the activities that children and their mothers normally enjoyed? How could he give her the answers she needed without breaking little Barbara's heart in the process?

In their drafty, two-room Chicago apartment, with the cold north wind rattling the windows, Bob May held his daughter in his arms and struggled to answer the child's simple question. He recalled the pain he had always felt growing up because he had been considered different. May had been a small, thin child, constantly picked on by other children, called "sissy" and other names he didn't want to remember. Even in college he was so slightly built that he was often mistaken for a boy.

Despite having a college degree, the country's sorry financial state had made it almost impossible for May to find any other job than the position at Wards that was far beneath his skill level. Yet when he found Evelyn and they fell in love and married, Bob suddenly felt like a king. For the first time he had a place in the world where it was all right to not fit the mold. Their daughter's birth seemed to assure the man that good times were just around the corner. But then Evelyn got sick and the cost of fighting the cancer stole not only his wife's energy but the family's savings as well. Bob sold everything of value and they lived in what amounted to a slum.

But on that cold, windy night, even with every reason to cry and complain, Bob wanted his daughter to somehow understand that there was hope . . . and that being different didn't mean you had to be ashamed. Most of all, he wanted her to know she was loved. Drawing from his own life experiences, the copywriter made up a story about a reindeer with a large, bright red nose. And as little Barbara listened, May described in story form not only the pain felt by those who were different but also the joy that can be found when someone discovers his special place in the world.

The tale was a big hit with Barbara, and thereafter she demanded that her father tell it to her each night. With every new telling the plot grew more elaborate, and the reindeer, Rudolph, became less a fictional character and more a member of the May family.

Unable to purchase a gift for Barbara that Christmas, Bob decided to carefully craft his story about Rudolph into a home-made book, drawing on his own abilities as an artist for the pictures. Many evenings after his wife and daughter had gone to sleep, Bob carefully worked to finish his unique present. But tragedy struck the May family before Christmas could arrive: Evelyn lost her battle with cancer.

Though the last few pages of his gift book were stained with tears, Bob would not give up on Rudolph. He knew that his daughter needed the uplifting story now more than ever. He prayed for the strength to finish the project. His efforts were rewarded when a thrilled Barbara found a completed copy of *Rudolph the Red-Nosed Reindeer* waiting for her on Christmas morning.

Though he hardly felt like celebrating, a few days later Bob was forced to attend a Montgomery Wards' employee party. His coworkers in the ad department asked May to share his children's story that night. Though he didn't feel like it, he took his book and, at the appointed moment, climbed before the crowd and read the story. After the scores of holiday revelers laughed, they stood and gave May and his children's tale a thunderous ovation. They all loved *Rudolph* and wanted copies of their own.

The head of the company felt that Wards could benefit from Bob's gift to his daughter. For a modest sum, Stewell Avery, the chairman of the board of Montgomery Wards, bought all rights from the cash-strapped and debt-ridden May. Avery then had tens of thousands of copies of *Rudolph* printed and shipped to Wards stores across the nation in time for Christmas 1939. The response was so positive that for the next six years, each child who visited a Santa in a company store got a copy of May's book.

By 1946 Wards had given away six million copies of *Rudolph* and Stewell Avery was being besieged by offers from every major publishing house wanting to print a new version of the story. In one of the most generous decisions ever made by the head of a large company, the CEO gave all rights back to Bob May. A year later the mass-market release of the book made the Wards copywriter a rich man.

With the book a best-seller, numerous toy and product deals were soon cut and May's entire life revolved around a story he had told to comfort a worried daughter. Remarried, and with a growing family, Bob couldn't imagine anything else that could improve his wonderful life. Then his brother-in-law, Johnny Marks, decided to adapt the story into a song.

Marks, who had written music for a number of major recording stars, hoped that the "Voice of Christmas," Bing Crosby, would record the song "Rudolph the Red-Nosed Reindeer." When Crosby passed, Marks offered the song to Dinah Shore. She wasn't interested either. Other artists were given the demo, but none of them wanted it. Finally cowboy star Gene Autry was approached. Marks figured that Autry might be looking for a follow-up to his earlier Christmas hit, "Here Comes Santa Claus." Besides, Gene, unlike Bing and Dinah, often sang kids' songs. Children were his main audience.

Like Crosby, Shore, and the other artists, Autry was unimpressed. He had already discovered a song he felt would become a seasonal children's classic in "If It Doesn't Snow This Christmas." There was no doubt that the favored title was a great song and a perfect children's single, but Marks begged Gene to give "Rudolph" a second listen. The writer figured that Autry might find a place for the misunderstood reindeer on the "B" side of the record.

Gene took Marks's demo home and played it for his wife, Ina. As they listened, Autry scoffed that there were already too many songs about reindeer. Ina thought differently. When she heard the line "they wouldn't let poor Rudolph play in any reindeer games," it broke her heart. She insisted that her husband cut the song.

Columbia Records wanted Autry to record four sides (songs) for a Christmas release. "Rudolph" was the last song chosen and cut. A few weeks later, when Autry sang "Rudolph" at the Madison Square Garden rodeo, the crowd went wild. As the cowboy's fans rose to their feet, the underdog deer flew past the other three new Christmas cuts and became the singer's holiday release for 1949. While Bing Crosby and Dinah Shore looked on, Gene Autry's "Rudolph the Red-Nosed Reindeer" streaked to number one on the charts. It would soon become the second best-selling Christmas song of all time, just behind "White Christmas."

Through books, records, television specials, and movies, for tens of millions of children of all ages, Rudolph has become as much a symbol for the secular wonder of the Christmas season as Santa Claus. While there are many lessons to be learned from this magical story—including that while it takes courage to be different, being different can be a blessing—there is an even greater lesson from this story and song that is now all but forgotten: When you give a sincere gift of love from the heart, that gift will come back to you magnified beyond all expectations and measures. It is a lesson that the fictional Rudolph and the very real May family are still living more than six decades after the story was first told.

25

SILENT NIGHT

*E*ven though "Silent Night" has been recorded more than any other song in history, the fact that we know it at all is a miracle. Created out of necessity and performed in a tiny village on a solitary Christmas Eve by two ordinary Austrians and a tiny choir, this incredibly beautiful and simple carol owes its debut to an organ that wouldn't play and a priest who wouldn't hold a Christmas mass without special music. Later, just weeks into the new year, the beloved carol's march to worldwide popularity was begun by the man who came to fix the faulty instrument.

In 1817, twenty-five-year-old Joseph Mohr was assigned to the position of assistant priest at St. Nicholas Church in Oberndorf, Austria. A lover of music since his boyhood in Salzburg, Mohr was placed in charge of the music used at the small church and he even wrote poems and song lyrics for special services. A seemingly tireless and giving man, he spent much of his spare time ministering to children from the area's poorest families. In his desire to serve and inspire, if ever a man fulfilled the full description of the word *pastor,* it was Mohr.

In 1818, during a particularly cold winter, Mohr was making last-minute preparations for a special Christmas Eve mass, a service he had been planning for months. Everything from music to message was in place. But as he cleaned and readied the sanctuary, the priest encountered an unfathomable dilemma: St. Nicholas's organ wouldn't play. A frantic Mohr struggled with the old instrument for hours, making adjustments, fiddling with keys, stops, and pedals, even crawling behind the console to see if he could find a problem. In spite of his efforts, the organ remained silent, its voice as still as a dark winter's night.

Realizing he could do nothing else, the priest paused and prayed for inspiration. He asked God to show him a way to bring music to his congregation on the year's most meaningful day of worship. Mohr would find the answer to his prayer born from events initiated almost two years before St. Nicholas's organ played out.

In 1816, while assigned to a church in Mariapfarr, Mohr had written a Christmas poem. The six unadorned stanzas were inspired on a winter's walk from his grandfather's home to the church. Though he had shared the words with a few friends, the priest never sought to have the work published nor attempted to come up with a melody to go with his words. When Mohr was transferred to the church in Oberndorf, he had brought the poem along with his few personal possessions.

Digging "Stille Nacht! Heilige Nacht!" from his desk, Mohr read over the words two years later. Up until that moment the verses hadn't seemed very important to the priest, but as he read them again, it was as if the Lord was tossing him a lifeline of hope. Bouyed by new and unfolding expectations, he shoved the worn paper into his coat pocket and rushed out into the night. Only hours before the Christmas Eve midnight mass, the priest fought his way through snow-covered streets.

※

On that same evening, thirty-one-year-old schoolteacher Franz Gruber was struggling to stay warm in his drafty apartment over the schoolhouse. Though he had once studied organ with noted teacher Georg Hardobler, he now played the instrument only for St. Nicholas's modest services. As he went over notes from one of his lessons, Gruber must have been surprised to hear an insistent knock at his door and find Father Mohr on the other side. By that time, the priest should have been at the church preparing for services, not making rounds, visiting old friends and colleagues.

After a quick "Merry Christmas," the obviously agitated priest pulled the teacher to the apartment's small table and signaled for Gruber to sit down beside him. In a distressed tone, Mohr explained the problem they faced. After he convinced Gruber nothing could be done to fix the organ, Mohr showed Franz his poem.

"Franz," he begged, "can you write music to these words that can be easily learned by our choir? Without the organ, I guess the song will have to be played on a guitar." The priest glanced at the clock on the table, and added, "The time is so short!"

Studying the poem, Gruber nodded his head. The look in his eyes and the smile on the schoolteacher's face showed that he felt up to the challenge. Confident again that God somehow had a special plan for this Christmas Eve, Mohr raced back

Silent night, holy night!
All is calm, all is bright.
Round yon Virgin, Mother and
    Child.
Holy infant so tender and mild,
Sleep in heavenly peace,
Sleep in heavenly peace.

Silent night, holy night!
Shepherds quake at the sight.
Glories stream from heaven afar
Heavenly hosts sing Alleluia,
Christ the Savior is born!
Christ the Savior is born.

Silent night, holy night!
Son of God love's pure light.
Radiant beams from Thy holy face
With the dawn of redeeming grace,
Jesus, Lord at Thy birth.
Jesus, Lord at Thy birth.

across the snow to the church, leaving Gruber alone with his thoughts, a ticking clock, and a prayer for inspiration.

❋

A few hours later the two friends met at St. Nicholas. There, in a candlelit sanctuary, Gruber shared his new music with Mohr. The priest approved, and after learning the guitar chords, rushed it to the choir members, who were waiting for their scheduled rehearsal. What should have taken weeks was accomplished in hours. In the little time they had, Mohr and Gruber taught the choir members the four-part harmonies to the last two lines of each verse.

Just after midnight, Mohr and Gruber stood in front of the main altar and introduced their simple little song. As they sang, they couldn't have guessed that "Stille Nacht! Heilige Nacht!" would be remembered not only the next Christmas in their small village, but almost two hundred years later, around the world.

A few weeks into the new year, Karl Mauracher, an organ builder and repairman from the Ziller Valley, traveled to Oberndorf to fix St. Nicholas's organ. While Karl worked, Mohr shared the story of how he and Gruber had used a guitar and an original composition to save the Christmas Eve mass. He sang the song he considered an answered prayer. Impressed, the repairman jotted down the words and learned the melody. Over the next few years, as he went about his profession, Mauracher introduced "Stille Nacht!" to many churches and towns.

During the nineteenth century, Austria and Germany had scores of traveling folk singers. Most of the groups were composed of family members who not only sang but worked specialized jobs to earn their keep as they journeyed from town to town. In 1832, the Stasser family folk singers appeared in a small community where Mauracher had recently installed an organ. During their stay, the family of singing glovemakers learned "Stille Nacht!" A few weeks later, at a concert in Leipzig, the Stassers performed the carol in front of a large crowd that had gathered for a fair. Moved by the song's deep spiritual message, King William IV of Prussia requested his nation's Cathedral Choir sing "Stille Nacht!" at his annual Christmas celebration. Due in part to the king's favor, "Stille Nacht!" stormed across much of Eastern Europe and pressed west to Great Britain.

In December of 1839, another Austrian family group, the Rainers, traveled to New York. As part of one of their performances, the family sang "Stille Nacht!" in English for a huge crowd at Trinity Church. It was such a popular number that other local groups began to sing it in churches. By the Civil War, "Silent Night" had become America's most popular Christmas carol. During the battle between the Union and Confederacy, it was not unusual for hostilities to cease for four days starting on December 25, with troops from both sides laying down their arms to come together to worship, share gifts, read Scripture, and sing "Silent Night."

As the carol's popularity spread, so did the legends about its origin. At various times music publishers gave composition credit to Beethoven, Bach, and Handel. It was only when Franz Gruber began a letter-writing campaign to newspapers and publishers, producing a copy of one of his first arrangements, that the true origin of "Silent Night" was finally recognized. Yet even with the melody's rightful

157

history secured, fanciful stories about the song's lyrics continued to spread.

Joseph Mohr died penniless in 1848, before being recognized as the carol's writer. Without the priest alive to refute the story, it became generally accepted that the song's lyrics had been written in haste after it was discovered that mice had chewed through the organ's bellows and disabled the instrument rather than the fact that it was old and simply broke in the extremely cold temperatures. Though a wonderful story and still accepted by millions, it is one of fiction much more than fact.

By the late 1800s "Silent Night" had been translated into more than twenty languages and was a vital part of Christmas celebrations all around the world. And by the twentieth century, like the celebration of Christmas itself, "Silent Night" had moved out of the church and into the mainstream.

❉

In 1905 the Haydn Quartet cut the first recording of "Silent Night." This first trip up the popular hit parade was just the beginning; literally thousands of others from around the world would record the simple carol in years to come. By 1960, the carol was recognized as the most recorded song in music history.

Despite its popularity, "Silent Night" remains in most minds what it was written to be—a simple, direct ode of praise. Created to make a Christmas service more meaningful, the old Austrian carol is as powerful and fresh today as it was on that first Christmas Eve it was sung at St. Nicholas Church. An answer to prayer, few words have better captured the story of a Savior born in a manger than "Silent Night."

26

SILVER BELLS

Jay Livington and Ray Evans rank as one of the most successful songwriting teams in history. With Livington composing the music and Evans writing the lyrics, the men scored time and time again with award-winning hits such as "To Each His Own" and "Another Time Another Place." By the early '50s, having already taken Academy Awards for "Buttons and Bows" and "Mona Lisa," they were two of the most sought after songwriters in the country; every movie studio, radio show, and recording artist wanted their latest offering. Though they scored with hundreds of songs and sales of their tunes climbed into the hundreds of millions, the two are now best remembered for a strange song about a horse and a beautiful ballad about Christmas. Both songs are so popular that most Americans of all ages can sing the words to them.

❋

In 1951 Bob Hope was one of the world's brightest stars. His name not only guaranteed big box office response at movie theaters, he already was a longtime radio star and had made a successful move to television. Beloved for his selfless work with U.S.O. tours in World War II and then Korea, Hope was "Mr. Christmas" to many members of the U.S. Armed Forces, even though he had never scored a hit with a Christmas song. From 1942 on, Bob spent every holiday season with men and women in uniform.

Paramount Pictures scheduled Hope to film a remake of the movie *The Lemon Drop Kid,* a perfect vehicle for his trademark humor. In the film, Hope would play a small-time gambler who owed a large sum of money to the mob. Unable to pay it off, the Kid would work a scam. In the midst of trying to outcon the cons, Bob's character would fall in love, reform, and escape a large number of near-fatal attacks. Of course, Hope would also find time to sing a song or two. With a cast of great characters surrounding the star, the cast and film crew began work in early 1951.

Livington and Evans, who had put together the wonderful score for Hope's box office smash *Paleface,* were called in to write the score for *The Lemon Drop Kid.* As they reviewed the script, they noted that it was a holiday movie with a new twist. *Holiday Inn, Christmas in Connecticut,* and a long list of other films had always been set in the country; now, for the first time in Hollywood history, songwriters were being asked to come up with a Christmas number that didn't embrace the pleasures of rural life during the holidays. It was a perspective American movies and songs had yet to explore.

After determining where music was needed, the songwriters had a brainstorming session in Evans's office. As they discussed the script, one of the men picked up a small silver bell and played with it. The tiny noisemaker magically transported the writers to the sidewalks of New York. As they began to think about the way streets and display windows were decorated, the attitudes of happy store managers and anxious shoppers, and the looks on expectant children's faces, the song they needed for Bob Hope and costar Marilyn Maxwell's duet quickly came together.

The team had been writing hits long enough to know when they had one, so Livington and Evans couldn't wait to take their latest work to the studio. But before the duo could share their latest composition with Bob Hope, they decided to sing it to Ray's wife. The men were chagrined and confused when the woman giggled as they sang. As she doubled over in laughter, the team wondered what had gone wrong.

When Mrs. Evans composed herself, she informed the duo that the chorus was all wrong. It wouldn't work, she assured them. She pointed out that when others heard it, they would laugh as hard as she had.

The song's problem could be traced to the small bell that served as its inspiration. Livington and Evans had named their song after that tiny instrument, and the song began, "Tinker bell, tinker bell, it's Christmastime in the city." As the writers once again listened to the words, they grinned along with Mrs. Evans. They quickly crossed out the word *tinker* and substituted the word *silver*.

When released, *The Lemon Drop Kid* was a moderately successful movie. Yet the film would have probably been quickly forgotten if not for the song "Silver Bells." Film patrons fell in love with it. This new genre of Christmas song fit well in the new America. After World War II, Americans had moved to urban areas in droves. This migration meant that more and more people were experiencing the bustle of holidays in cities than ever before. Livington and Evans's unadorned descriptions of everything from stoplights blinking red and green (the yellow caution light had not yet been added) to thousands of shoppers rushing from store to store struck a chord with millions who were exposed to those things every day. The bells that anchored the chorus were everywhere too. They rang in cathedral towers, jingled along horse-drawn carriages, and were constantly chiming in the hands of men and women seeking donations to help feed the poor and needy. In the city, bells, much more than anything else, signaled the coming of the holiday season. "Silver Bells" fully captured this experience in song.

Bob Hope may have introduced "Silver Bells" to the world, but it was his friend Bing Crosby who cashed in on the song's market potential. Bing recorded the hit version of the Livington-Evans collaboration, and soon everyone else seemed to be recording the hit too. When President John F. Kennedy declared it his favorite Christmas song, "Silver Bells" rang out loudly in the White House. By the year 2000, hundreds of different versions of the song had rung up more than 150 million record sales, proving that JFK wasn't the only one who embraced this sentimental holiday offering as a favorite.

After completing *The Lemon Drop Kid*, Bob Hope continued to sing "Silver Bells" to U.S. troops at Christmas for more than four decades. His work in Vietnam and other combat arenas helped make him the most honored private citizen in United States history. Hope's holiday entertainment junkets to the far parts of the globe also earned him the label of "the G.I.'s Santa Claus."

Though they could have retired and lived on the royalties from their Christmas hit, Jay Livington and Ray Evans continued to write. In 1956 they won their third Oscar for "Que Sera Sera" and scored again with the title song from *Tammy*. Yet it was the theme song for a very unique television series that ranks right up there along with "Silver Bells" as their most remembered work. The same writing duo that composed the incomparable "Mona Lisa" and incredible "Silver Bells" also gave the world the whimsical and silly theme from "Mr. Ed."

THERE'S A SONG IN THE AIR

*I*n the summer of 1904, Karl P. Harrington was working on the most important assignment he had ever been given. The teacher, composer, and church music director was helping to assemble a new Methodist hymnal. As he reviewed hundreds of familiar songs previously published in other songbooks, Harrington carefully considered the task at hand. In between the covers of the hymnal had to be songs that would address every worship need of countless different congregations. That meant he had to include music that could be sung by huge church choirs in places like Boston and by tiny congregations in places like Salem, Arkansas. Every pastor and song leader would be depending upon the songs included; other than the Bible itself, his project would be the most important tool found in most churches. The missionary task of leading the lost to Christ—and inspiring the saved to work for the Lord—would be helped or hindered by the songbook. Even for a man of Harrington's education and experience, the job he faced was overwhelming.

The middle-aged Harrington had been chosen for the project because he had studied at a dozen different colleges in the United States and Europe. A talented organist, he knew worship music well and had penned several original songs while also developing new arrangements for dozens of recognized works. As a Wesley University music professor, he had the time to properly study thousands of songs and consider their merits. Yet even though his hours spent with students gave Harrington a new perspective and energy, his months employed studying hymns and making cuts in the hymnal seemed to zap his vigor and strength. *Why have I accepted this job?* he must have wondered. *What chance do I have of satisfying the needs of everyone who picks up the songbook? Can I find one song that will touch all those who use this hymnal?*

Harrington loved to read; it was one of the ways he relaxed. In an attempt to get away from the demands of his work, the teacher often turned to one of his favorite authors, Josiah Holland. As he toiled over the hymnal, his reading of Holland's works became more and more of a refuge.

❄

Josiah Holland was born in 1819 in Massachusetts. After trying to master the new art of photography, Holland went to college and became a doctor. Soon, however, his love for literature exceeded his passion for medicine. By the time he reached the age of forty, he had given up his practice and was on the staff of the *Springfield Republican*. A few years later he founded *Scribner's* magazine. While editing the prestigious monthly, Holland began to write novels. His works of fiction reflected his own moral upbringing. In each of his heroes readers found strong figures who might have been tempted, but never strayed far from the straight and narrow.

In the midst of turning out several best-selling books, Holland also wrote poetry. A deeply religious man, the editor used the story of the first Christmas to create a poem for an 1874 Sunday school journal. "There's a Song in the Air" combined a sweetness and majesty rarely found in holiday verse. The way the writer mixed the image of a young mother, her new baby, the events of the birth, and the revelation that this child was the King of all creation was indeed inspired. Yet this unique view of Christ's birth might have been lost if the author hadn't decided to reprint it in an 1874 book entitled *Complete Poetical Writings*. Three decades later, more than twenty-five years after Holland had died, it was *Complete Poetical Writings* that Karl Harrington chose to help him escape from the rigors of finding songs for a hymnal.

It was a hot summer day when Harrington wiped the sweat from his brow as he turned the pages of Holland's book. Taking a sip of a cool drink, the teacher read the next poem. As he silently studied the words, his eyes lit up. Holland's works were usually casual and distant, but this one was aflame with vigor and energy. When he finished "There's a Song in the Air," Harrington took a deep breath and read the poem again. *This needs to be put to music,* he thought. *This piece needs to be sung by Christian voices everywhere!*

There's a song in the air!
  There's a star in the sky!
There's a mother's deep prayer
  and a baby's low cry!
And the star rains its fire while
  the beautiful sing,
For the manger of Bethlehem
  cradles a King!

There's a tumult of joy over the
  wonderful birth,
For the virgin's sweet boy is the
  Lord of the earth.
Ay! the star rains its fire while
  the beautiful sing,
For the manger of Bethlehem
  cradles a King!

In the light of that star lie the
  ages impearled;
And that song from afar has
  swept over the world.
Every hearth is aflame, and the
  beautiful sing
In the homes of the nations that
  Jesus is King!

We rejoice in the light, and we
  echo the song
That comes down through the
  night from the heavenly
  throng.
Ay! we shout to the lovely evan-
  gel they bring,
And we greet in His cradle our
  Savior and King!

Going over to the organ, Harrington again studied the words to "There's a Song in the Air." This time he read them aloud, forming a tune around each phrase. As his fingers touched the keyboard, a melody came to life. On an oppressively hot summer day—much like Torme's "The Christmas Song," written almost forty years after it—a great Christmas song was born.

In 1905, Karl Harrington's music was officially married to Josiah Holland's poem in the first printing of *The Methodist Hymnal*. An answer to a professor's prayer, "There's a Song in the Air" became the perfect song for large and small churches, as well as one of the most beautifully crafted carols ever written.

THE TWELVE DAYS OF CHRISTMAS

*F*or millions, "The Twelve Days of Christmas" is nothing more than a novelty song. Most link this old Christmas carol with other nonsensical numbers such as "Grandma Got Run Over by a Reindeer" or "I Saw Mommy Kissing Santa Claus." Yet even though this song seems to make little sense now, there was a time in England when "The Twelve Days of Christmas" was once one of the most important teaching tools of the Catholic church.

Beginning in the sixteenth century, British Catholics were forbidden by law to practice their faith. The only legal Christian denomination in the British Empire was the Church of England. Those Catholics who spoke or wrote of their faith were arrested and tried under the laws of the time. If their violation was considered severe enough, they were either hung or drawn and quartered. Children as well as adults were subject to the same laws, and age did not prevent the state from dealing harshly with even a young practitioner of the faith.

In the face of persecution and death, millions refused to abandon the religion of their ancestors. So, much like the early Christians in Rome, Catholics in England went underground. They held secret masses, studied their doctrine behind closed doors, and hid all signs of their faith at home. They were an almost secret society.

One of the most severe problems the Catholic underground faced was in teaching their children the doctrine of the church. Since writing down anything dealing with the Catholic faith could cost both writer and reader their lives, the messages of doctrine and faith had to be reproduced in secret code. One of the most successful codes ever invented by the Catholic underground during the period was a Christmas carol that on the surface appeared to make no sense at all. Ironically, this rather strange ode became so popular that it found its way into pubs, concert halls, and even the royal palace. Few, certainly not the king or the head of the Anglican church, suspected that the meaning behind the song's lyrics included some of the most important elements of doctrine of the outlawed Catholic church.

When it first became popular, many in England tried to explain that the meaning of "The Twelve Days of Christmas" could be found not in the presents, but in the days. There were several theories based on this explanation, ranging from the theory that the verses represented the days leading up to December twenty-fifth to the explanation that the words embraced a gift-giving celebration lasting a dozen days after Christmas Day. During discussions in regard to which days the song referred, the meaning of the unusual gifts were most often passed off as the fancies of a young man sick with love—the argument being that the gifts made no real sense because men in love rarely thought or acted logically. Yet nothing could have been farther from the truth; the gifts were the clue to unlocking the code.

On the first day of Christmas,
My true love gave to me,
A partridge in a pear tree.

On the second day of Christmas,
My true love gave to me two
    turtle doves.
And a partridge in a pear tree.

On the third day of Christmas,
My true love gave to me three
    French hens.
Two turtle doves
And a partridge in a pear tree.

On the fourth day of Christmas,
My true love gave to me, four
    calling birds . . .

On the fifth day of Christmas,
My true love gave to me five
    gold rings . . .

On the sixth day of Christmas,
My true love gave to me six
    geese a-laying . . .

On the seventh day of Christmas,
My true love gave to me seven
    swans a-swimming . . .

On the eighth day of Christmas,
My true love gave to me eight
    maids a-milking . . .

On the ninth day of Christmas,
My true love gave to me nine
    ladies dancing . . .

On the tenth day of Christmas,
My true love gave to me ten
    lords a-leaping . . .

On the eleventh day of Christmas,
My true love gave to me eleven
    pipers piping . . .

On the twelfth day of Christmas,
My true love gave to me twelve
    drummers drumming . . .

The days were a simple mark of the time between Christ's birth and the Epiphany, the time when the wise men came to honor the newly born king. They were nothing more. The secret meaning for Catholic boys and girls was found not in the dozen days, but in the very special gifts. As the children sang, they weren't to think of the actual gifts, but of something much different.

Every Catholic child was taught that only pure and true love came from God. So from the beginning of "The Twelve Days of Christmas," each singer understood that this song was about a heavenly love, not about a boy's crush on a girl.

The importance of Christ's death and resurrection was the anchor to the faith—and to the song—and was therefore repeated with each new verse. The single partridge in a pear tree represented courage and devotion above what man ever showed on earth. A mother partridge lures enemies away from her defenseless chicks in order to protect them. Just as she sacrifices her own life for her children, so did Christ for us. Add to that image a pear tree that symbolized the cross and, together, this first gift represented the ultimate gift given by the Babe born on Christmas Day.

The second gift, two turtle doves, stood for both the Old and New Testaments of the Bible. Doves were also symbols of truth and peace, once again reinforcing the tie to Christ and Christmas.

Today three French hens mean nothing, but in the sixteenth century they were very expensive food items reserved for only the richest homes. If a banquet served French hens, then it was truly a meal fit for a king. In the song, the hens symbolized the expensive gifts brought by the wise men. When Catholic children sang the third verse of the song, they pictured not chickens, but gold, frankincense, and myrrh.

The four calling birds stood for the authors of the Gospels that trumpeted the story of Jesus and told about his life and ministry from birth to death. In a very real sense, the birds' names were Matthew, Mark, Luke, and John.

In keeping with the biblical theme, the five rings stood for the five Old Testament books that Christians knew as the "law of Moses" and Jews refer to as the "Torah." These gifts were to remind the singer of not only man's fall from grace due to sin, but the fact that a Savior would come to offer salvation and a path back to God.

"Six geese a-laying" might have seemed comical to those who sang the song without knowledge of the phrase's true meaning, but to underground Catholics this symbolic code was easily understood and incredibly logical. The Lord made the world in six days. Just as eggs are the symbol for new life and creation, so the geese laying eggs presented the whole story of God moving his hand over the void to create life.

"Seven swans a-swimming" would have been a huge mystery to the uninformed as well. Paul's writing in Romans 12:6–8 speaks of the "gifts of the Holy Spirit." These gifts—prophesy, service, teaching, encouraging, giving, leadership, and mercy— were linked to the lyrics' symbol of the swans, birds considered by many to be the most graceful and beautiful fowl in England. Catholic children were thus taught that when you walked with God, the gifts of the Spirit moved in your life as easily as a swan on water.

"Eight maids a-milking" represented the common man whom Christ had come to serve and save. At the time the song was written, no job in England was lower than working with cattle or in a barn. For a female servant to be used in this way indicated that she was of little worth to her master. Yet Christ, the King of Man, served people without regard to status, race, sex, or creed. The number eight in this verse also represented the beatitudes listed in Matthew 5:3–10: blessed are the poor in spirit, those who mourn, the meek, the hungry, the merciful, the pure of heart, the peacemaker, and the righteous.

In the verse that followed, the fruits of the Spirit—love, joy, peace, patience, kindness, goodness, faithfulness, gentleness, and self-control—were hidden by the image of nine ladies dancing. It truth, this dance taught the real joy and rewards of serving Christ.

"Ten lords a-leaping" represented the Ten Commandments. Since a lord was supposed to be a just and honorable man and the final voice of law in his domain, it was understandable why ten lords would represent the ten laws God gave his people through Moses.

There were twelve disciples, but in the end one of them did not embrace Christ or his message of salvation. The eleven pipers piping thus served as the image of the eleven apostles who took the message of Christ's life and resurrection to the world.

The final gift, twelve drummers drumming, represented a very important confessional taught to all Catholics. Called the "The Apostles' Creed," the confession contained a dozen different elements. The drum was probably used as a symbol of the pace or rhythm that this creed gave each believer's daily walk with the Lord. The Apostles' Creed, familiar to even many non-Catholics, reads:

I believe in God the Father, maker of heaven and earth, in Jesus Christ, his only Son, our Lord, conceived by the Holy Spirit, born of the Virgin Mary. Who suffered under Pontius Pilate, was crucified, died, and was buried, descended into hell; the third day he rose from the dead, ascended into heaven and sits at the right hand of God, the Father Almighty. He shall return to judge the living and the dead. I believe in the Holy Spirit, the holy catholic church, the communion of saints, the forgiveness of sins, the resurrection of the body, and life everlasting.

It is doubtful that the English Catholics who composed and taught this song to their children would have wanted the true meaning of "The Twelve Days of Christmas" to be hidden forever. When the practice of Catholicism was no longer a crime in England, those who had created the song probably wished that its mysteries be revealed. Yet by the time Britain freed the Catholic faith, the words had taken on a life of their own and no one seemed ready to link the seemingly shallow song with other carols that spoke directly of the birth of the Savior. Even today, four hundred years later, though "The Twelve Days of Christmas" has been recorded hundreds of times and performed hundreds of thousands of times, few can sing the song without laughing at its unusual message and the air capacity it takes to get through it. Perhaps the fun that masked its original intent is why "The Twelve Days of Christmas" has survived for so long, as well as why the Catholic church survived oppression in merry old England.

29

WE THREE KINGS OF ORIENT ARE

*I*n the second chapter of the book of Matthew there is a brief passage that reads, "There came wise men from the east to Jerusalem." Who were these men? Most, including King Herod, thought they were astrologers. That is how they are identified in the Bible. When they informed Herod they were looking for the "king of the Jews," it caused panic in the royal court and ultimately led to the murder of countless baby boys throughout the land of Israel in an attempt to kill a future threat.

While Herod struck terror throughout the land in his search for the baby Jesus, the wise men found the child by following a star to Bethlehem. According to the gospel of Matthew, they threw themselves at the infant's feet and worshiped him, presenting him with gifts of gold, frankincense, and myrrh. Then, without reporting back to Herod, they departed for home, never to be heard from again.

What many call the commercialization of Christmas—the practice of giving gifts—can probably be traced back to the wise men's presents that very first Christmas. Beyond that fact, nothing else is really known about the wise men. Still, despite a lack of concrete knowledge, a host of writers and theologians have drawn some very detailed pictures of the famous travelers over the past twenty centuries.

The consensus of opinion among most serious Bible scholars is that the astrologers came from Persia. The fact that astrologers in that land were often priests is probably why they are often called Magi. The Magi were, in fact, dream interpreters for the Persian royal family. Though they often worked within the confines of the royal palace with the kings of the country, these wise men were not of royal blood and not even members of the ruling caste. So if they were Persian star readers, they could not be kings.

How many wise men made the journey to Israel in search of Jesus is another question that has been answered more by imagination than documentation. No one really knows how many there were. Because the text in Matthew clearly records wise "men," there were obviously at least two. The three wise men so often mentioned in stories and songs probably resulted in the fact that Matthew told of three gifts brought by the wise men to Jesus. The number of gifts, however, had nothing to do with how many wise men had brought them; the gifts were symbolic of the important three areas of Christ's life—the gold representing his kingly reign, the frankincense symbolizing his ministry, and the myrrh foreshadowing his death and resurrection. There could have been as few as two wise men or as many as a dozen or more.

Writers of the Middle Ages not only extrapolated about number, but even made "educated guesses" at names. By 1500 millions of Christians could tell you not only that the three men's names were Caspar, Balthazar, and Melchoir, but also that this trio of gift bearers were actually kings. While from a historical perspective this made little sense, it did add something special to many of the imagined tales that sprang forth over the next four hundred years.

※

Three kings or not, the story of the wise men was the focal point of the post-Christmas celebration of Epiphany. In many places the holiday, observed on January 6, once rivaled Christmas. Since the celebration of Epiphany has declined over the past century, many today don't know what it is. Literally, Epiphany is the last of the twelve days of Christmas, the day the wise men finally found Jesus.

The Episcopal Church celebrated Epiphany in both America and the United Kingdom. During the 1800s the special day was traditionally the day the Christmas tree was taken down and children received the gifts and treats that had been hanging on it since it had been cut, brought home, decorated, and had presents hung on the branches. Even then, as many little ones counted the moments until they could raid the evergreen, a great number of them didn't know the symbolism behind Epiphany or why gift-giving was a part of it.

Though he had no children of his own, thirty-seven-year-old John Henry Hopkins Jr. enjoyed the childlike spirit of the Christmas season he saw in observing his nephews and nieces. A brilliant scholar, with degrees from the University of Vermont and a law school in New York City, he was still a child at heart. And as an ordained priest in the Episcopal church, he did not wear his clerical collar at the time, favoring his own writing over preaching from a pulpit. Upon graduating from seminary and law school, Hopkins picked up his pen to become a reporter for a New York newspaper. He then continued his

We three kings of Orient are
Bearing gifts we traverse afar,
Field and fountain, moor and
    mountain,
Following yonder star.

Chorus:
O star of wonder, star of light,
Star with royal beauty bright,
Westward leading, still
    proceeding,
Guide us to thy perfect light.

Born a King on Bethlehem's
    plain
Gold I bring to crown Him
    again,
King forever, ceasing never,
Over us all to reign.

Chorus

Frankincense to offer have I;
Incense owns a Deity nigh;
Prayer and praising, voices raising,
Worshiping God on high.

Chorus

Myrrh is mine, its bitter perfume
Breathes a life of gathering gloom;
Sorrowing, sighing, bleeding,
    dying,
Sealed in the stone cold tomb.

Chorus

Glorious now behold Him arise;
King and God and sacrifice;
Alleluia, Alleluia,
Sounds through the earth and
    skies.

Chorus

career as a scribe with the New York–based *Church Journal*. He was writing for that publication in 1857 when he confronted a special problem—the conundrum of what Epiphany gifts he should purchase for his brothers' children. Ultimately, Hopkins decided to give a present that would both entertain and educate at the same time.

Having decided on his gift, Hopkins sat down at his desk with a single goal in mind: to write a moving tribute to the legendary visitors from the East described in the gospel of Matthew. To accomplish this mission, the writer imagined what it might have been like to be one of the wise men. A seminary graduate, he was aware that little was known about the travelers, so he combined the biblical record of the trip with the legends passed down over almost two thousand years.

Though largely a work of the imagination, the song that was produced as Hopkins's gift to his nephews and nieces was instructive and worshipful. The cadence of his melody fully captured the image of a trip across the desert and plains on camels. The carol had an oriental, Middle Eastern feel to it and its rhythm reflected the beat of a march or the sway of a camel's gait.

Hopkins's words dramatically embraced the rich fabric of the trip, the gifts, and the birth of a Savior. Using simple, but inspired lyrics, the writer initially described the quest to find the king. Though the first verse contains only four short lines, they speak of a trip that was long and difficult: "bearing gifts we traverse afar." The chorus, with its powerful view of a "star of wonder, star of light" guiding the wise men onward, provided the inspiration the men needed to not give up during the arduous and perilous journey.

The second verse begins the tale of a "king forever ceasing never" born in Bethlehem. Hopkins's wise men realized that this king has not been born to rule a short time but for eternity. The composer therefore reveals that the three men were as wise as they were strong and courageous.

In the last part of the second verse and the following two stanzas, the gifts presented by the wise men are fully covered. Each gift is identified and the meaning of the gift told with almost biblical eloquence. The gold is the crown that the king would forever wear. The frankincense is there to help worship the Son of God. The myrrh is the bitter perfume that would mask death but then blossom forth in a life unending.

In the song's final verse, Hopkins assures the youngest members of his family that the three wise kings knew that the Christ child would die for our sins and then be born again. In the last stanza, the writer reveals that to these three kings the journey was truly divine, worth every effort, and the most glorious moment of their lives. It not only defined their lives and purpose, it made them an important part of the most amazing story ever told.

Hopkins's "We Three Kings of Orient Are" was published in the writer's own songbook, *Carols, Hymns, and Songs*. At the turn of the next century, when many churches decided that carols should be included in hymnals, this musical work, which defined the reason for the celebration of Epiphany, became one of America's most popular Christmas songs.

John Henry Hopkins Jr. never married or had a family of his own. Yet because he loved children, he'd be pleased to know that his most famous Christmas song is one of the most beloved children's carols in the world. He probably wouldn't even mind that on many occasions the lyrics to "We Three Kings of Orient Are" have been rewritten in several humorous ways. What he would surely want every child to know is that Christmas gifts began not in a department store or a catalog but on the twelfth day of the first Christmas, when three men from the East brought gifts to the baby Jesus. Though many have now forgotten the celebration of Epiphany, John Henry Hopkins Jr.'s "We Three Kings of Orient Are" will never allow us to forget what the wise men brought to celebrate the birthday of the King of kings.

30

WHAT CHILD IS THIS?

What Child Is This?" one of the most moving and beautiful Victorian carols, can trace its history back farther than the days of the infamous Henry VIII. Though the song was registered to a Richard Jones in 1580, legend has it that the notorious King Henry might have even written the original lyrics himself as he courted Anne Boleyn. The song's association with King Henry was forever tied to "Greensleeves" when William Shakespeare used it in his play *The Merry Wives of Windsor*.

The haunting melody, often associated with guitar or harpsichord solos, most likely predates Henry VIII by hundreds of years. As an ancient English folk song, there have been more than twenty different known lyrics associated with it throughout history and many more might have been lost. First published in 1652, the melody became even more popular than the lyrics associated with Henry VIII.

For much of its early life, the tune known as "Greensleeves" was associated with pubs as a popular drinking song.

Although God is mentioned in a closing verse of the best-known lyrics, nothing about the song closely resembled a religious piece; it was simply one of the era's most popular folk songs. By the nineteenth century "Greensleeves" was almost as beloved as "God Save the Queen." Even without its association with Christmas and "What Child Is This," "Greensleeves" would probably still be a well-known tune in England today. Yet it was with different lyrics that the world fully embraced the British tune.

William Chatterton Dix was assuredly not thinking about "Greensleeves" when he sat down with pen and paper to record his thoughts of Christmas in 1865. Dix was an insurance man by trade, but a poet at heart. Serious about his writing, he studied other poets, read classic literature, and spent a great deal of time in college working on his creative craft. The Englishman was even named after Chatterton, one of England's greatest poets. Dix's father, who insisted that William be christened with the scribe's name, had once written a biography of the poet and encouraged his son to follow in the footsteps of his hero.

Born in Somerset, England, in 1837, during a time when few adventurous folks migrated more than fifty miles from their place of birth, Dix found himself manager of a marine insurance company in Glasgow, Scotland, by the time he was twenty-five. Though in charge of some of his company's most important accounts and eventually the head of a growing family, Dix still found time to write. Many correctly accused him of pursuing poetry as his passion and his job as a sideline venture.

Dix's writing embraced a wide range of thoughts and subjects. It lacked much focus, however, until tragedy struck. A near-fatal illness robbed him of his strength and confined the man to bed for many months. As he lay near death, he often reflected on his faith. Reading his Bible and studying the works

What child is this, who, laid to rest,
On Mary's lap is sleeping?
Whom angels greet with anthems
    sweet,
While shepherds watch are keeping?
This, this is Christ the King,
Whom shepherds guard and angels
    sing:
Haste, haste to bring him laud,
The babe, the son of Mary.

Why lies he in such mean estate
Where ox and ass are feeding?
Good Christian, fear: for sinners here
The silent Word is pleading.
Hail, Hail, the Word made flesh,
The babe, the son of Mary

So bring him incense, gold, and
    myrrh,
Come, peasant, king, to own him.
The King of kings salvation brings,
Let loving hearts enthrone him.
Joy, Joy for Christ is born
The babe, the son of Mary.

of respected theologians, Dix reaffirmed his belief in not only Christ as Savior but in the power of God to move in his own life. Not long after regaining his strength, an inspired Dix produced some of the greatest hymns ever written by an English layman. Songs by Dix such as "Alleluia! Sing to Jesus!" and "As with Gladness, Men of Old," are still being sung all around the world today.

In the era while Dix was writing hymns and raising a family, Christmas was not the commercial celebration it is today. Neither was it a season where many openly celebrated the birth of Christ. Conservative Christian churches forbade gift-giving, decorating, or even acknowledging the day. These Puritan groups feared that if set aside as a special day, Christmas would become a day of pagan rituals more than a very serious time of worship. Other churches held services but were also intent on the day being reserved for only a time of worship. In this context it was unusual for Dix to feel moved to write about Christ's birth, since many hymn writers of the period ignored Christmas altogether.

There is no record of why Dix decided to write of the first Christmas, nor did he share with his friends and family how the poem he penned was written quickly in a single session. Yet the writer's Christmas work, entitled "The Manger Throne," quickly emerged as his most memorable effort.

The song's powerful words presented a unique view of the birth of Christ. While the baby was the focal point of the song, the viewpoint of the writer seemed to be that of an almost confused observer. In a stroke of brilliance, Dix imagined visitors to the humble manger wondering who the child was that lay before them. Employing this special perspective, the author wove a story of the child's birth, life, death, and resurrection. Each verse also answered with a triumphant declaration of the infant's divine nature.

Dix published "The Manger Throne" in England just as the U.S. Civil War was ending. Perhaps because of the fragile state of America's collective spirit, bruised and torn by four years of fighting, "The Manger Throne" was quickly imported from Britain to the United States and became a well-known Christmas poem in both the North and the South. Yet while it was used in church services and printed in magazines and newspapers, it wasn't until an unknown Englishman coupled Dix's lyrics with the melody "Greensleeves" that the carol became immensely popular on both sides of the Atlantic. Unlike many others who penned lyrics to now-famous holiday classics, Dix, who died in 1898, lived long enough to see "The Manger Throne" become the much beloved Christmas carol "What Child Is This?"

Though Dix's inspired words are now recognized as some of the most concise yet powerful ever used in a hymn, it is in reality the old English tune "Greensleeves," with the advent of radio and recording, that allowed "What Child Is This?" to continue to grow in popularity. Once the unique melody is heard, "Greensleeves" is seldom forgotten. Soulfully touching and beautiful when sung a cappella or accompanied by a lone guitar, it is also awe-inspiring and soaring when arranged for a cathedral choir or an orchestra. Perhaps that is why William Dix's song remains as one of the most beloved and remembered of all Christmas carols.

WHITE CHRISTMAS

erhaps no single voice signals the beginning of the Christmas season like that of Bing Crosby. By the same token, no modern secular Christmas song means as much to so many as does "White Christmas." Many believe that Christmas just isn't Christmas until they have heard Crosby sing "White Christmas." In a very sincere and simple manner, this carol seems to say more with fewer words than anything ever written about holidays in America.

Bing Crosby was born in Tacoma, Washington, in 1901. Thirty years later Crosby, who had been working as an entertainer since he left home as a teen, landed a CBS radio contract and began recording for the Brunswick label. His first number one hit, "Out of Nowhere," from the film *Dude Ranch*, initiated an unparalleled string of best-selling singles and launched a film career that spanned decades. With record sales of more than three hundred million, Crosby remains today one of the top vocal acts of all time. When his record sales are combined with his success on radio, television, and in movies, it can be argued that Bing was the most important single entertainer in the history of show business.

Crosby was raised in a Christian environment and was a religious man. Not only did he know most of the familiar Christmas carols by heart, he had been singing them since his youth. In the midst of the Great Depression, Bing, by then recording for Decca, went into the studios determined to put a facet of his faith on wax. Singing with the Guardsmen Quartet, Crosby's "Silent Night, Holy Night" surprised everyone, topping out at number seven on the hit parade charts. Over the course of the next few years, the single sold more than ten million copies. The Christmas hit was Bing's seventy-ninth charting single; it became the most successful record of his early years, working its way back into the top ten again in 1938. For his fans, it was also the first concrete step in forever linking the singer to the holidays.

Crosby's continued musical and movie successes proved a gold mine to the singer, his record label, and Paramount Pictures. This success also meant that the world's very best songwriters were beating a path to Bing's door. One of those who would come to pen a lot of Crosby hits was a man named Irving Berlin.

If Crosby was the nation's premier singer, then Berlin was his composing counterpart. Other tunesmiths might have been more sophisticated or even more talented, but no one had their finger on the nation's pulse like Berlin. He knew what Americans wanted; he sensed their dreams and their fears. And most remarkably, he was able to turn this knowledge into marvelous stories in song.

Born as Israel Baline in Mohilev, Russia, Berlin spent his youth in New York City. In 1911, while working as a waiter and pitching tunes on the famed Tin Pan Alley, Irving wrote

"Alexander's Ragtime Band." Thanks to that song, Berlin suddenly found himself, at the age of twenty-three, in the spotlight. With talent, drive, and ambition, he stayed in the public's eye for the next eight decades. The writer's list of hits fills pages, but if he had only penned "Blue Skies," "God Bless America," and "There's No Business Like Show Business," he would still be remembered today as an entertainment giant. His legendary status was sealed in 1941 when he was asked to score a motion picture that starred Bing Crosby and Fred Astaire.

The film, *Holiday Inn*, was typical of Hollywood musical formula—a hero wanting to live a dream faces failure time and time again, and while searching for success, he falls in and out of love. The plot had been used on countless occasions in movies and Broadway, but this film's hook was unique in that the musical score and story line tied it to the holidays.

Facing the task of writing about the day Americans loved to celebrate, Berlin's genius became evident again. He drew on his own experience and observations, a formula that seemed to work for him every time. As always, he composed easy-to-remember lyrics and melodies that went straight to the heart. Yet he was having a problem with one song in the movie; as a Jew, writing something for Christmas demanded insight he didn't feel he had. But Berlin didn't beg off or turn the job over to someone else. With marked determination, he continued to toil over his assignment.

As Berlin worked on his Christmas song, he considered what he *did* know of the holidays. As a New Yorker, when he thought of the season, he pictured snow and Santa. Yet as he spent many holiday seasons working in Los Angeles, he was well aware that for many, what made the atmosphere of Christmas special was more of a nostalgic dream than a reality; across America, everyone wanted that perfect white day when "treetops glisten" and children anxiously await Santa's arrival. Everyone knew that the only Southern California location where it was ever going to snow was on a Hollywood sound stage. Using this premise as an anchor, he wrote what was to become the pivotal song for *Holiday Inn*—the song that would make the movie a classic.

When he finished his work, Berlin was not sold on the effort; he even thought about tearing the piece up and starting over. But before he did, the disappointed writer took the time to sing it to Crosby. Bing loved it and convinced Berlin not to change anything about the tune he called "White Christmas."

Crosby first sang the song on his December 25, 1941 radio show. Perhaps because it was a sober Christmas, just three weeks after the United States had been forced to enter World War II, the performance generated instant response. Bing recorded it six months later. Just after *Holiday Inn* hit theaters in late summer, Decca released Crosby's "White Christmas" as a single. Driven by both the movie and family separations caused by the war—thousands of soldiers were far from home, longing for the familiar sights and sounds of the holidays— the song topped the charts for twelve weeks. The tune about which Irving Berlin had such misgivings would go on to win the Academy Award for best song of 1942.

Over the course of the next twenty years, Bing Crosby's "White Christmas" landed on the charts fifteen more times. It hit number one again in 1945 and 1946. Crosby's version eventually sold more than thirty million records and spawned a successful motion picture of the same name. The song's incredible sales alone indicate that of all the modern Christmas songs, "White Christmas" simply and eloquently best voices the Christmas dreams and wishes of most Americans. The song scores because, no matter where we are, we want to see snow on Christmas Day. For a few hours, we want our Christmas to look like a greeting card. The chord Berlin somehow struck and Crosby's voice echoed captures the childlike longings in every person who truly loves the holidays and the spirit that makes them special.

Bing Crosby died in 1977. Just before his death, he filmed a television special that was to air during the Christmas season. With his family around him, the man whose voice had for so long signified the beginning of the holidays sang "White Christmas" for the last time. There could not have been a better way for the singer—who charted more than 350 times—to say farewell. As long as children press their faces to the window looking for Santa, families make plans to get together for holiday dinners, and folks dream of snow on Christmas day, there will always be a place for Bing Crosby's "White Christmas."